I0478856

Cornwall Ontario in Colour Photos, Saving Our History One Photo at a Time

Photography
by Barbara Raué
2016

Series Name:
Cruising Ontario

Book 154: Cornwall

Cover photo: 36 Fourth Street West, Page 40

Series Name: Cruising Ontario
Saving Our History One Photo at a Time
in colour photos

Books Available in Alphabetical Order:
Aberfoyle, Acton, Alton, Amherstburg, Ancaster, Arthur, Aylmer, Ayr, Bloomingdale, Brantford, Burlington, Caledon, Caledonia, Cambridge, Clifford, Conestogo, Delhi, Dorchester to Aylmer, Drayton, Drumbo, Dundas, Eden Mills, Elmira, Elora, Essex, Fergus, Guelph, Hagersville, Hamilton, Hanover, Harriston, Hespeler, Jarvis, Kingston, Kingsville, Kitchener, Linwood, Listowel, London, Lucknow, Mono, Mount Forest, Neustadt, New Hamburg, Niagara-on-the-Lake, Oakville, Orangeville, Orillia, Owen Sound, Palmerston, Peterborough, Petrolia, Port Elgin, Preston, Rockwood, Sarnia, Seaforth, Sheffield, Shelburne, Simcoe, Southampton, St. Jacobs, St. Marys, St. Thomas, Stoney Creek, Stratford, Thamesford, Tillsonburg, Waterdown, Waterford, Waterloo, Welland, Wellesley, Windsor, Wingham, Woodstock

Book 114-116: Waterloo updated
Book 117-119: Windsor
Book 120-121: Amherstburg
Book 122: Essex
Book 123-124: Kingsville
Book 125-127: Woodstock
Book 128: Thamesford
Book 129-132: St. Marys
Book 133-136: Sarnia
Book 137: Petrolia
Book 138-139: Welland
Book 140-145: Kingston
Book 146-149: Ottawa
Book 150-151: Midland

Book 152: Penetanguishene
Book 153: Kemptville
Book 154: Cornwall
Book 155: Mariatown to Maitland
Book 156: Morrisburg

Other Books by Barbara Raue

Coins of Gold

Arrows, Indians and Love

The Life and Times of Barbara
Volume 1: Inventions That Have Enhanced My Life
Volume 2: Entertainment That I Have Enjoyed
Volume 3: East Coast Trips
Volume 4: Olympics Have Always Intrigued Me
Volume 5: Wonders of the World
Volume 6: Caribbean Cruises We Have Enjoyed
Volume 7: Animals
Volume 8: Storms and Other Major Disasters in My Lifetime
Volume 9: Wars, Terrorist Attacks and Major Disasters

The Cromwell Family Book

Laura Secord Discovered

Daddy Where Are You?

Montana Series
Book 1: Montana Dream
Book 2: Life on the Montana Frontier
Book 3: Montana to Boston and Back

Visit Barbara's website to view all of her books
http://barbararaue.ca

Table of Contents

Cornwall is Ontario's easternmost city, located on the Saint Lawrence River about one hundred kilometres southeast of Ottawa. It is named after the English Duchy of Cornwall. It is the seat of the United Counties of Stormont, Dundas and Glengarry.

In June 1784, disbanded Loyalist soldiers and their families settled at New Johnstown, the site of present day Cornwall. Native traders and French missionaries and explorers came here in the 17th and early 18th centuries. By 1805 Cornwall had a court house, a schoolhouse, two churches and many homes. The construction of the Cornwall Canal in 1834-42 accelerated its development. Mills and large factories were erected along the canal.

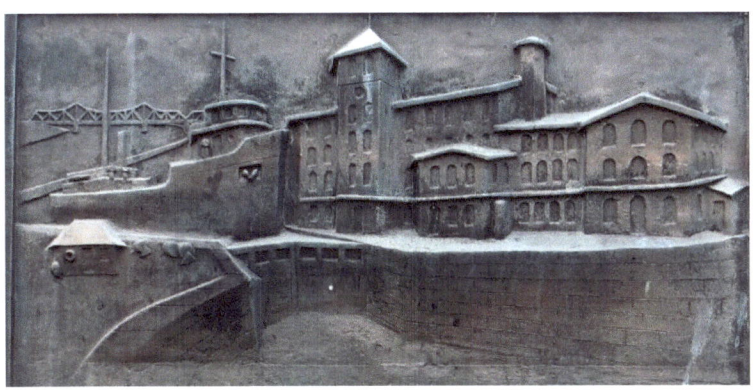

The Cornwall Canal, a series of locks which carried boats18.5 kilometres around the rapids, was used for over one hundred years. Power drawn from the canal attracted textile and paper mills. The textile industry played a major role in Cornwall's economic and cultural development. This canal was one of eight canals that connected western Canada with the ocean by way of the Great Lakes and the St. Lawrence River. The Canal was an important shipping centre until the completion of The St. Lawrence Seaway in 1959.

Eastern Ontario has always been a highway or corridor through which people moved, a corridor used by migration and conquest. Prior to European colonization, the Mohawks and Six Nations Iroquois settled and raided through the St. Lawrence valley. The French and British fought over the waterway and, after the American Revolution in 1812–14, it became a battleground between Americans and Canadians. Formally founded to be a new home for refugees, it remained a home for refugees and migrants for much of its history.

Slavery was ended in the colony of Upper Canada in stages, beginning in 1793 when importing slaves was banned, and culminating in 1819 when Upper Canada Attorney-General John Robinson declared all slaves in the colony to be freed, making Upper Canada the first place in the British Empire to unequivocally move towards abolition.

The aftermath of the American Revolution resulted in the formal division of Upper and Lower Canada (later Ontario and Quebec) to accommodate Loyalists fleeing persecution in the new United States, and distribution of land throughout Southern Ontario brought major change to Eastern Ontario.

The original 516 settlers arrived with minimal supplies and faced years of hard work and possible starvation. Upon their departure from military camps in Montreal, Pointe Claire, Saint Anne, and Lachine in the fall of 1784, Loyalists were given a tent, one month's worth of food rations, clothes, and agricultural provisions by regiment commanders. They were promised one cow for every two families, an axe, and other necessary tools in the near future. For the next three years, bateaux (boat) crews delivered rations to the township, after which residents were left to fend for themselves.

Cornwall was unusually integrated for a town in Ontario. For hundreds of years, the local population has been characterized by a mix of economic migrants, refugees and opportunists. Mixing of different social classes and ethnic backgrounds was common even early in its history, due to the interdependence demanded by isolation and the lack of support or interference from authorities.

In the 1780s to1830s, a "Bee" was a social event that pooled local labor resources, and was often a festive occasion. These "Bees" drew on many different classes, backgrounds and ethnic and linguistic groups working together for survival. These were very common in Eastern Ontario generally, and especially so in the early villages of the St. Lawrence valley.

Cornwall was once home to a thriving cotton processing industry. Courtaulds Canada, Inc.'s rayon manufacturing mill operated until 1992. Domtar, a Quebec-based company, operated a paper mill in the city for nearly 100 years, ceasing operations in 2006. Cornwall's industrial base has now shifted to a more diversified mix of manufacturing, automotive, high tech, food processing, distribution centers and call centers.

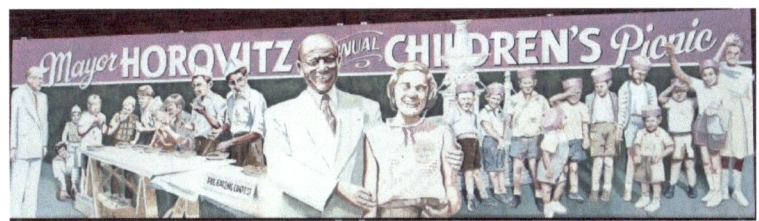

Horovitz Park – mural on northwest corner of Pitt and First Streets – The 1940s were the years of Cornwall's favourite mayor, Mayor Horovitz. He promoted community involvement and hosted an annual picnic in the park.

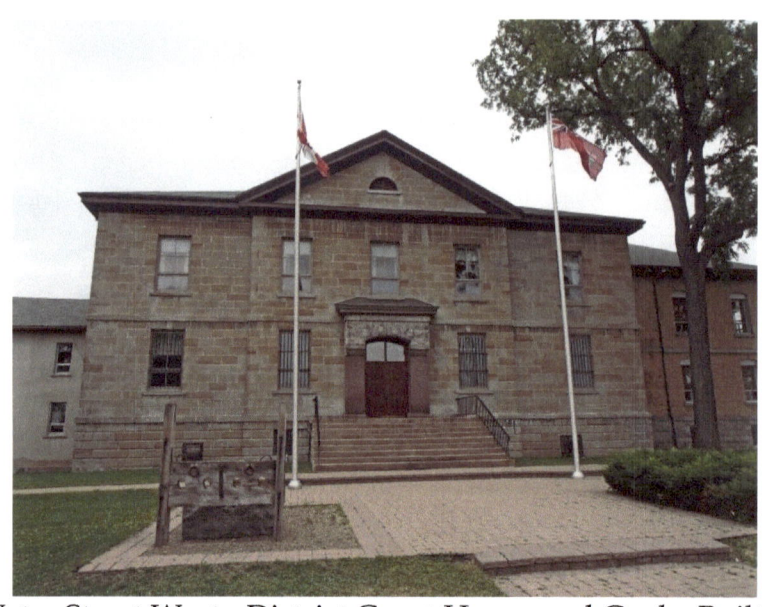

11 Water Street West - District Court House and Gaol – Built in 1833, the jail operated until 2002. The cell blocks, common areas, exercise yard and visitation area have been maintained as they were when they were populated by inmates sentenced to jail time.

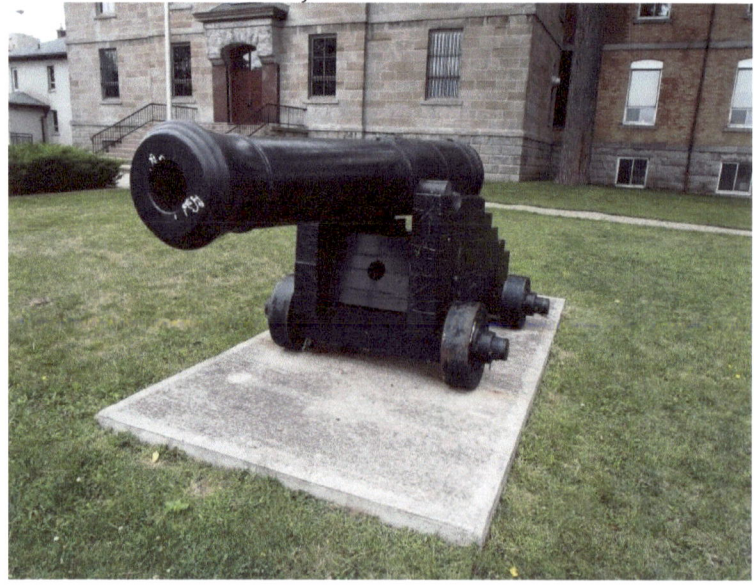

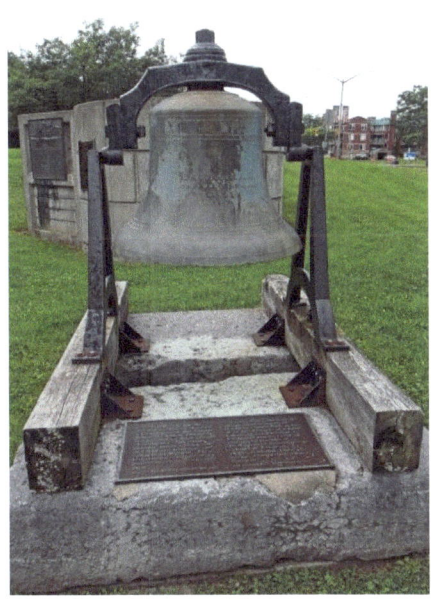

This bell rang out the different parts of a working day for employees at the Canada Mill at the foot of Edward Street and provided an alarm in case of emergencies. The bell remains a symbol of an industrial era in Cornwall's past.

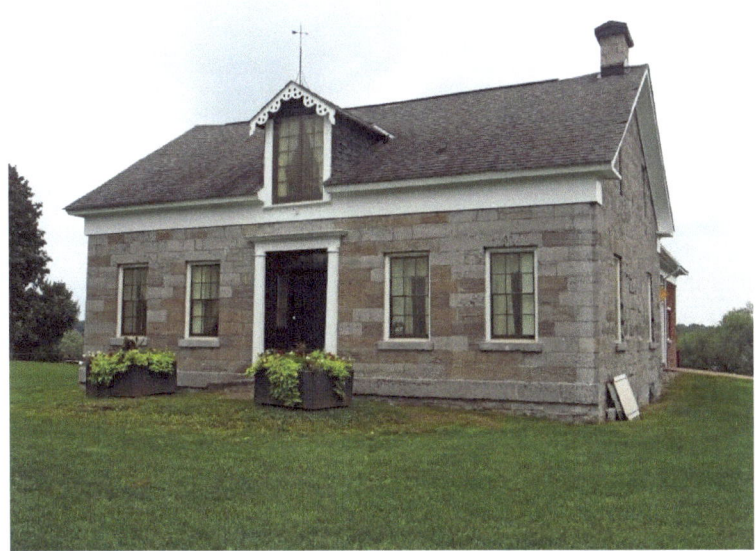

160 Water Street West – Wood House – 1840 – stone homestead – now Cornwall Community Museum

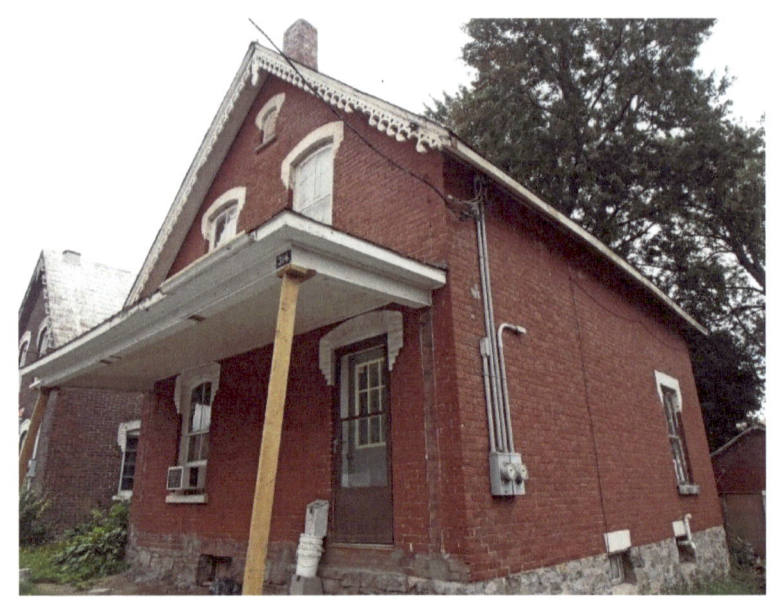

314 Water Street East – Gothic – verge board trim on gable
with finial; voussoirs

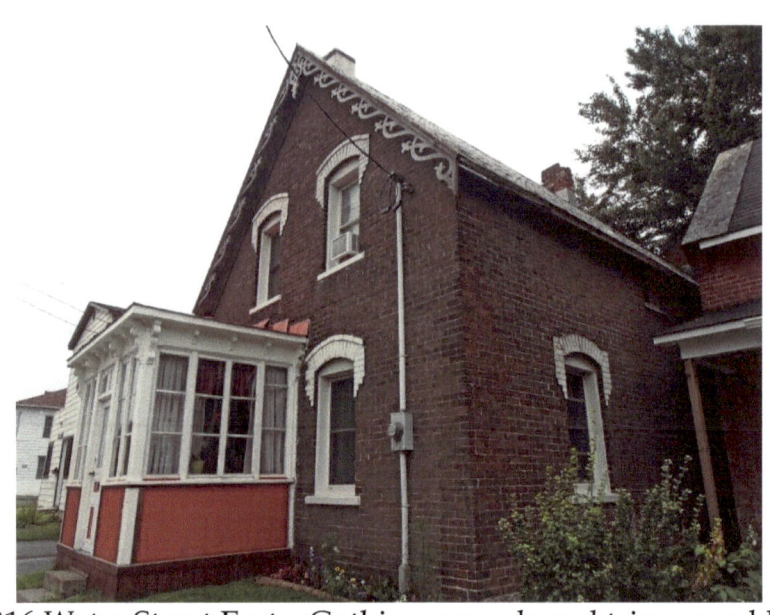

316 Water Street East – Gothic – verge board trim on gable
with finial; voussoirs; enclosed entrance porch added

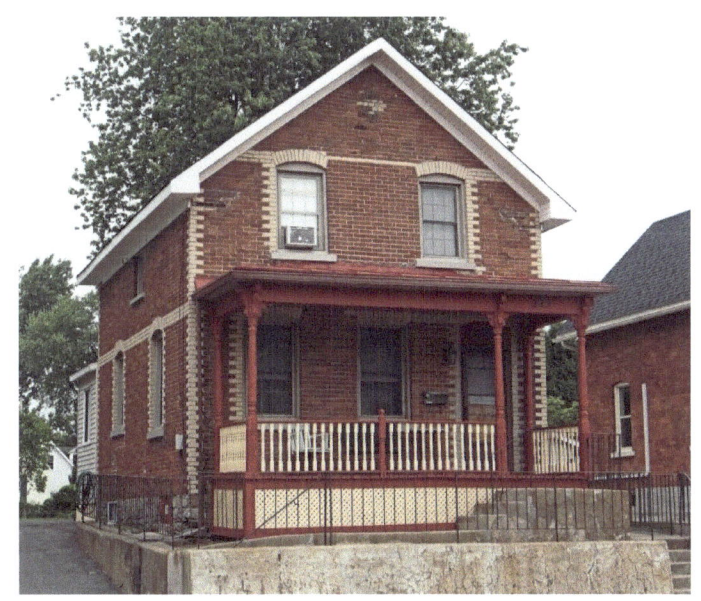

325 Water Street East – Gothic – dichromatic brickwork, corner quoins, banding

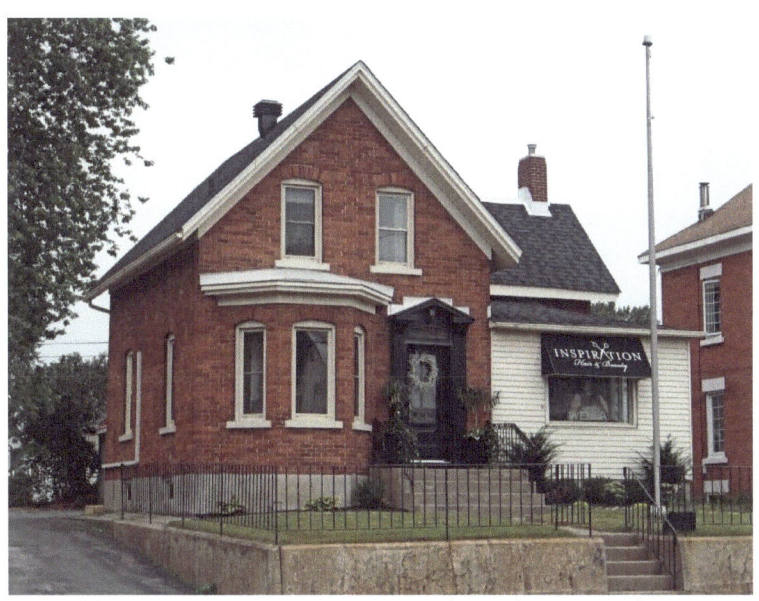

331 Water Street East – Gothic - bay window

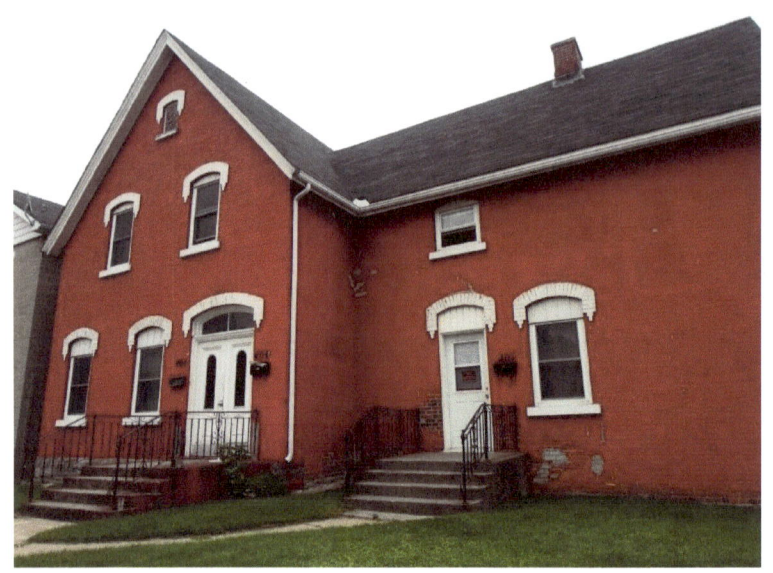

402-404 Water Street - voussoirs

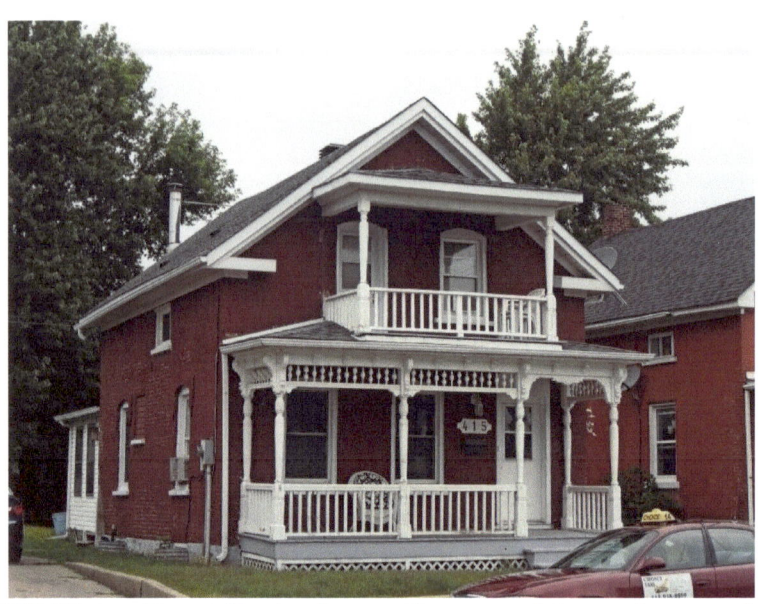

415 Water Street East - decorative wood-turned veranda support posts, open railing; second floor balcony; cornice return on gables

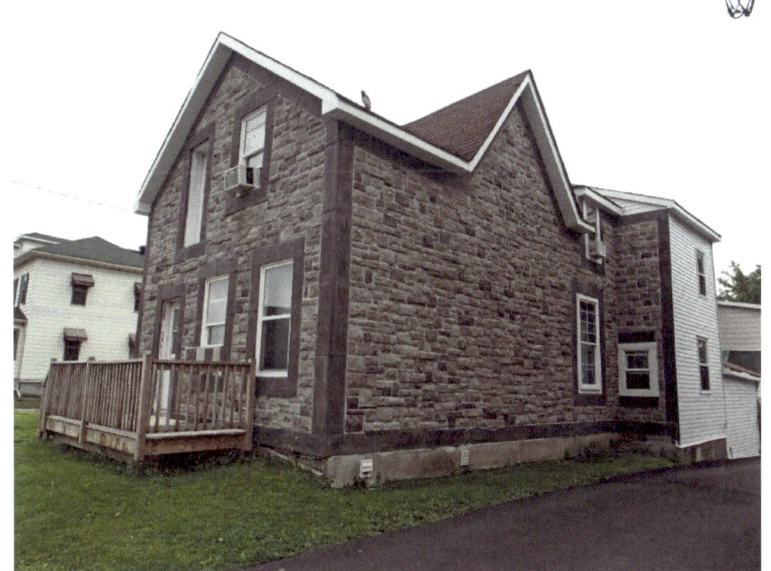

418 Water Street East – Gothic - stone

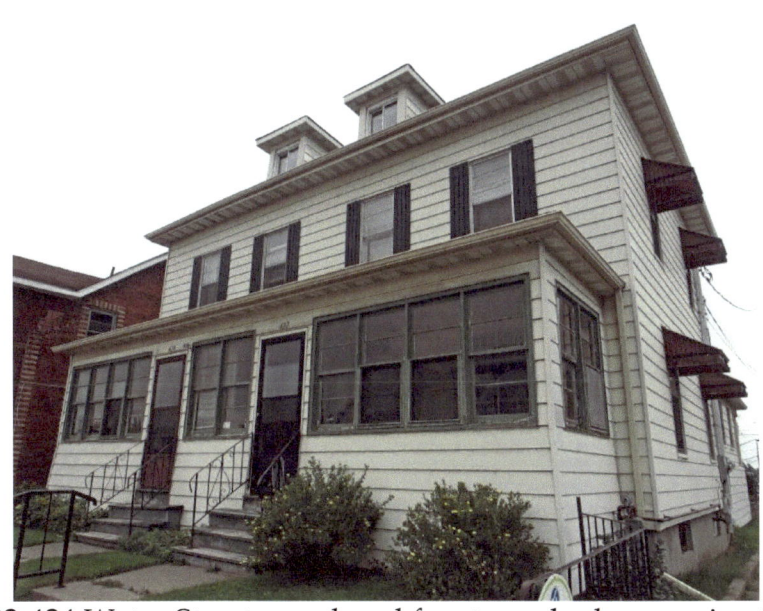

422-424 Water Street – enclosed front porch; dormers in attic

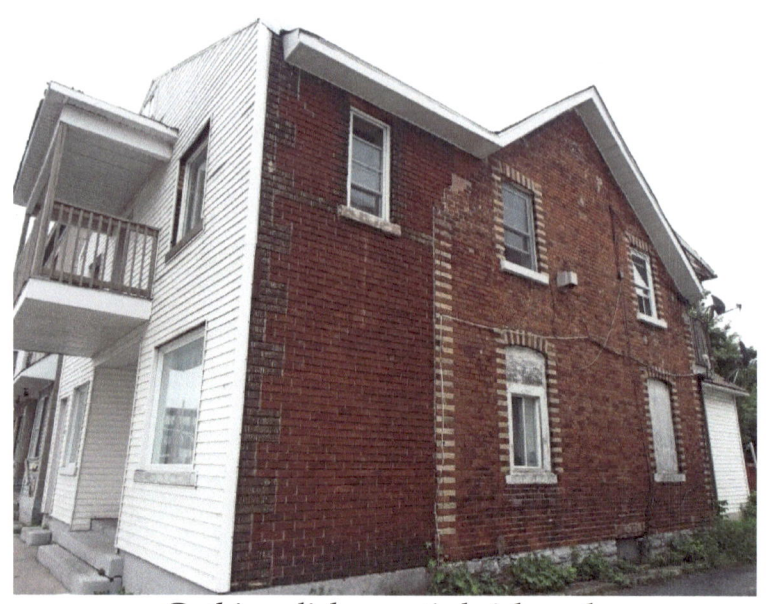

Gothic – dichromatic brickwork

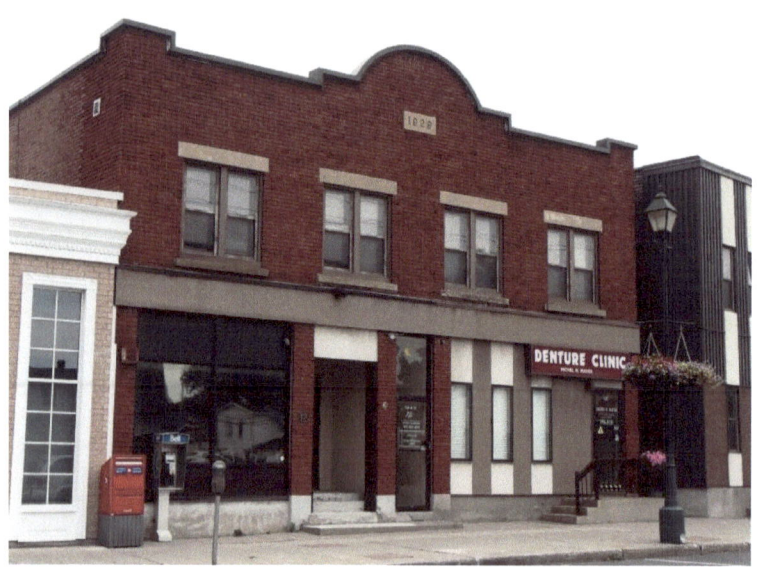

12 Marlborough Street – 1929 – Jacobean gable

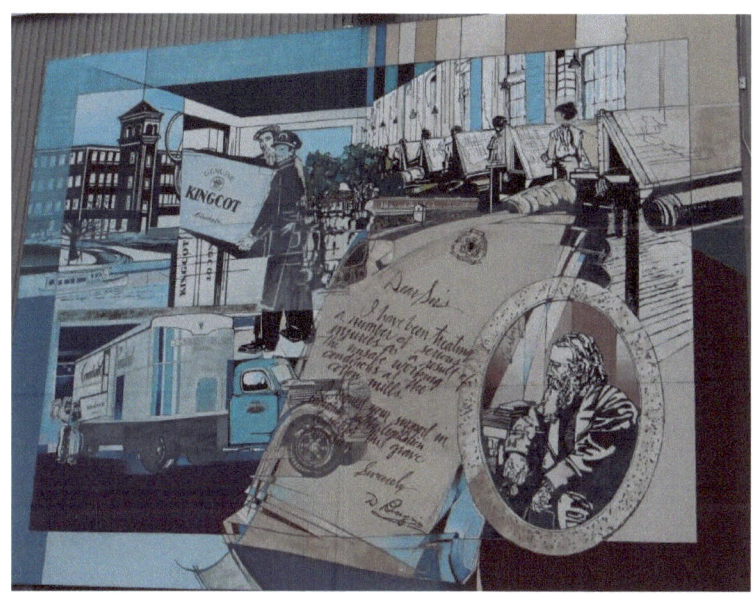

The Cotton Industry – mural corner of Montreal Road and Albert Street - The cotton industry sustained Cornwall's economy from 1880-1959. The three factories: Stormont, Dundas, and Canada. Work in the mills was very dangerous. Dr. Darby Bergin was elected as MP who petitioned for industrial safety. The cotton mills were the second set of factories to be lit with Thomas Edison's electric system.

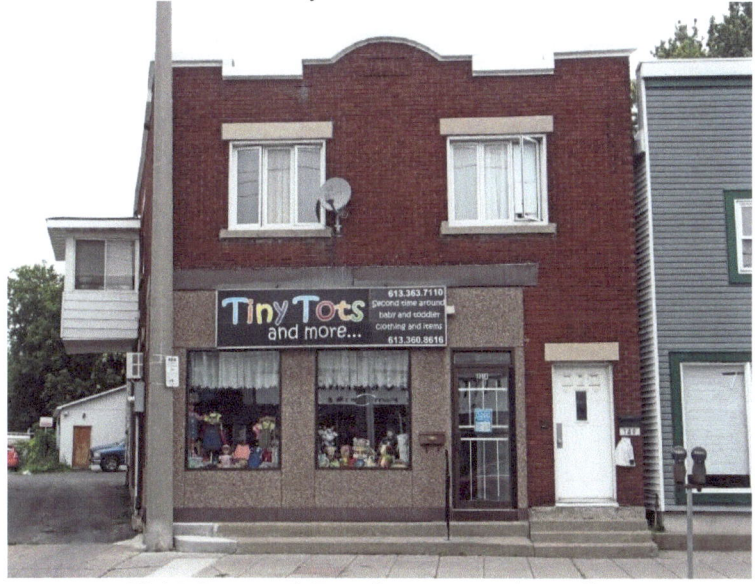

136 Montreal Road – stepped roofline

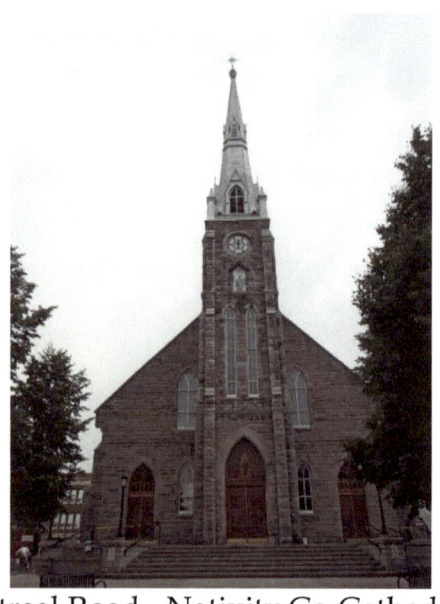

300 Montreal Road - Nativity Co-Cathedral - 1891
(A co-cathedral is a cathedral church which shares the
function of being a bishop's seat with another cathedral, often
in another city) - Gothic - imposing south façade, with its high
stone tower and spire; buttressed stone walls, pointed arches
of the lancet windows and doors

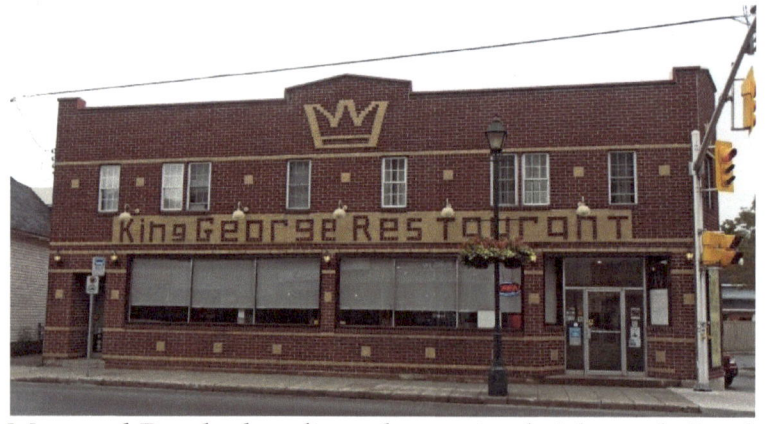

401 Montreal Road – banding, decorative brick work, Jacobean
gable with a crown in the brickwork

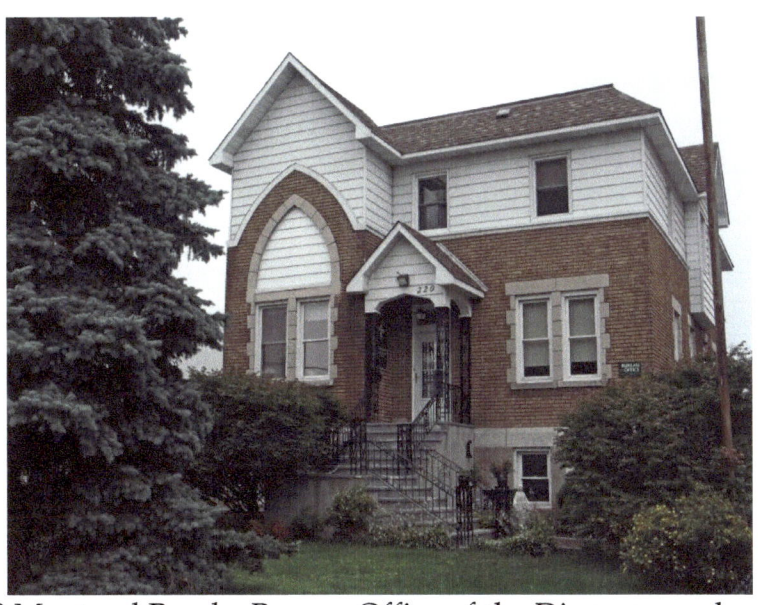

220 Montreal Road – Bureau Office of the Diocese – arch over window with blind tympanum, open pediment above door

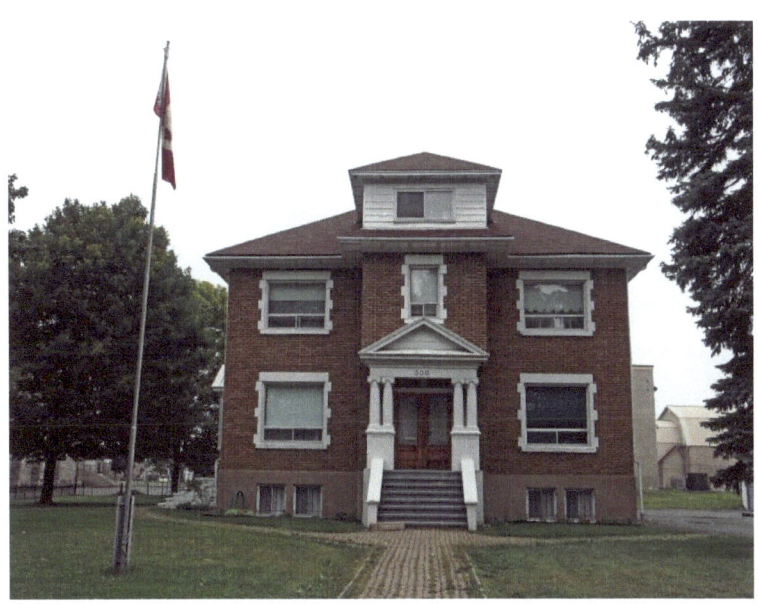

300 Montreal Road – Italianate – hipped roof with dormer; pillars with Ionic capitals; pediment; quoining around windows

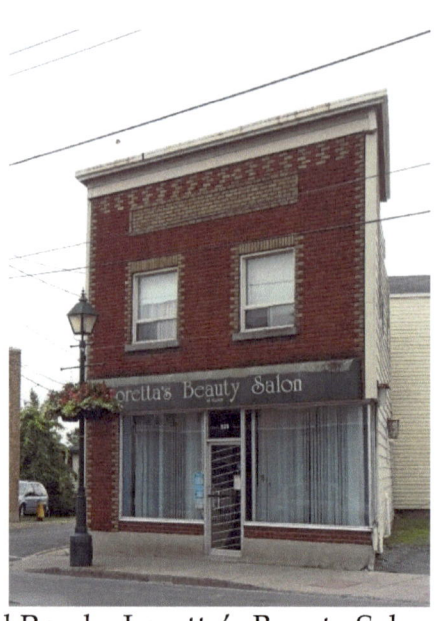

528 Montreal Road – Loretta's Beauty Salon – decorative dichromatic brickwork, corner quoins

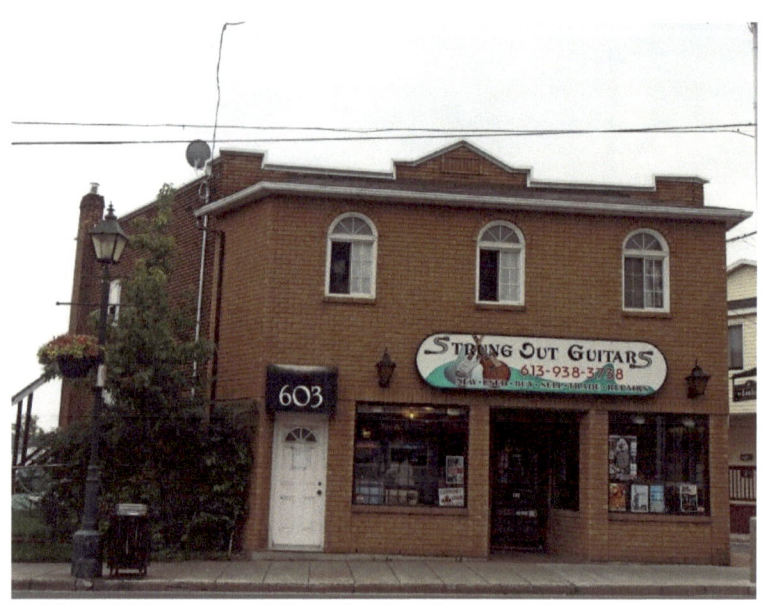

601-603 Montreal Road – Jacobean gable; voussoirs

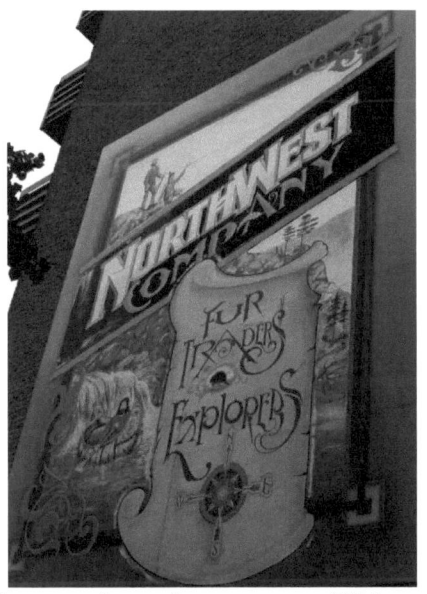

The Fur Trade mural on the corner of Edward Street and Montreal Road

Two people who had a significant impact on the development of Canada settled in this region: Simon Fraser and David Thompson. Simon Fraser was involved in the fur trade; he moved to Upper Canada as a Loyalist during the American Revolution; he was employed by the Northwest Company in 1792 and he later became a partner in the company. David Thompson was a cartographer who charted the vast expanse of Canada's North West.

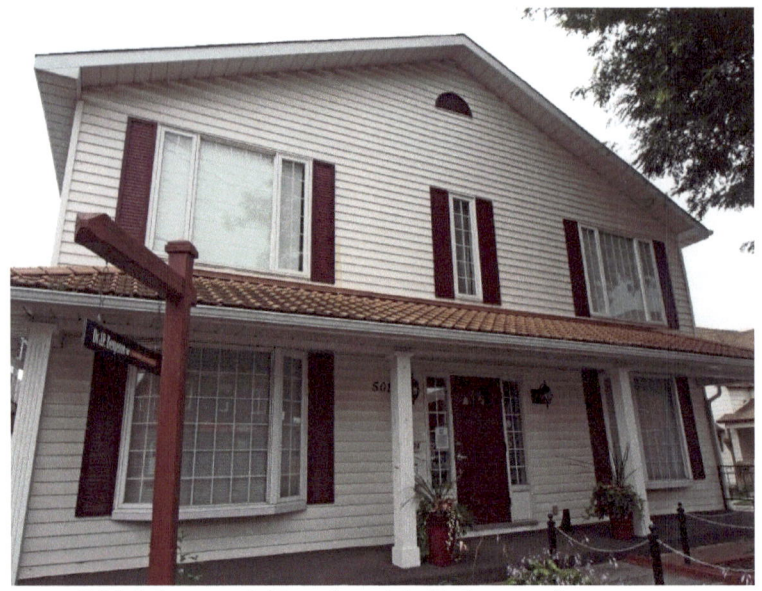

501 Montreal Road – sidelights and transom

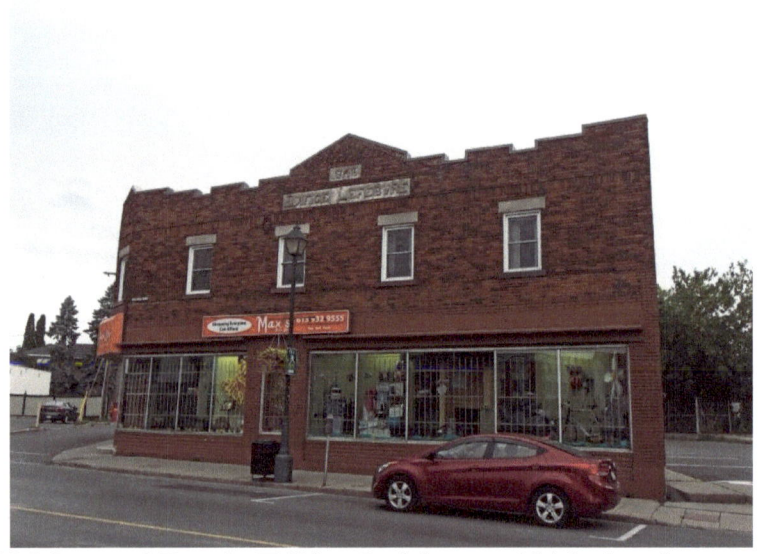

500 Montreal Road - Edifice Lefebvre – 1946 – battlemented roofline with center Jacobean gable; decorative brickwork

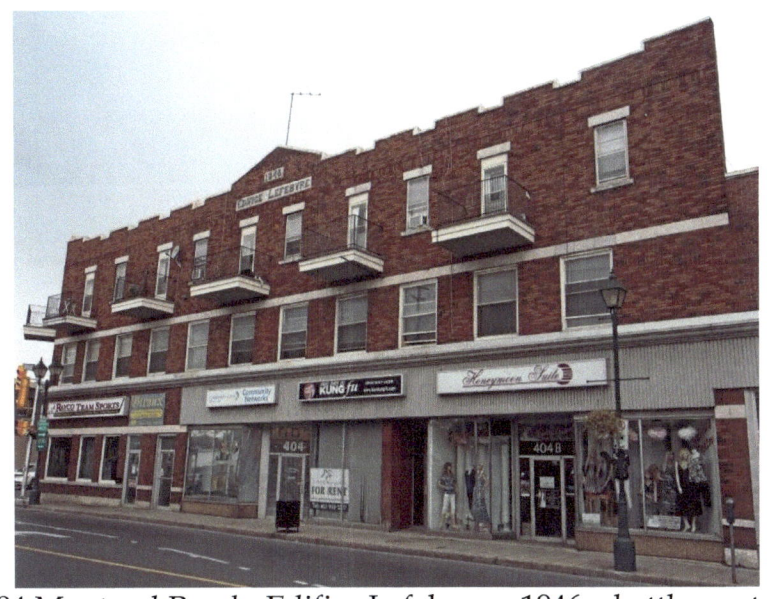

404 Montreal Road - Edifice Lefebvre – 1946 – battlemented roofline with center Jacobean gable; second floor balconies; decorative brickwork

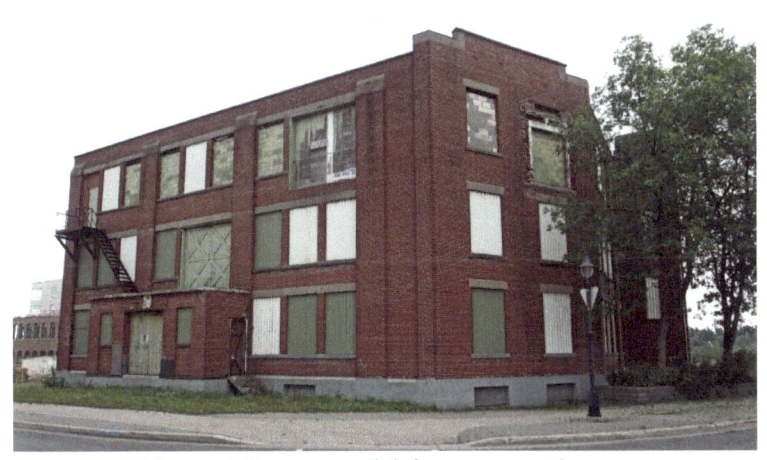

Edward Street – old factory - pilasters

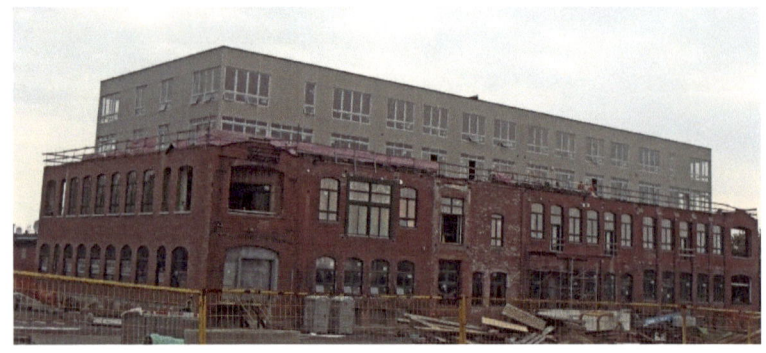

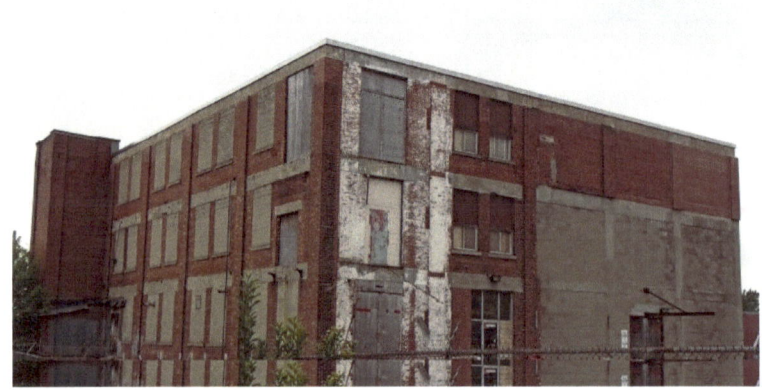

Edward Street – old factories

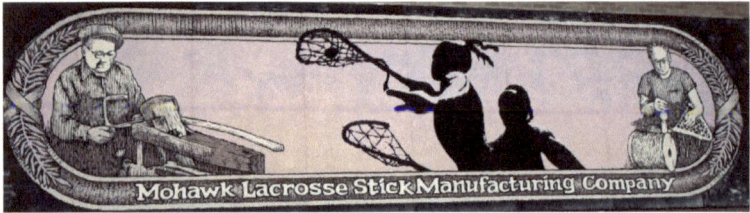

Mohawk Lacrosse Stick Manufacturing Company mural on south wall of Cornwall square – lacrosse was Canada's national winter sport until 1994 (replaced by hockey)

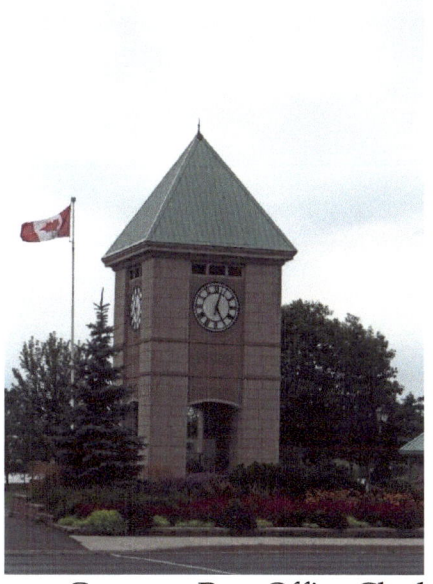

Pitt Street - Gateway Post Office Clock tower

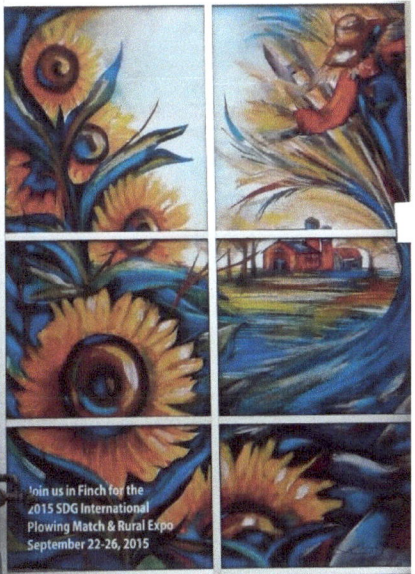

Window painting

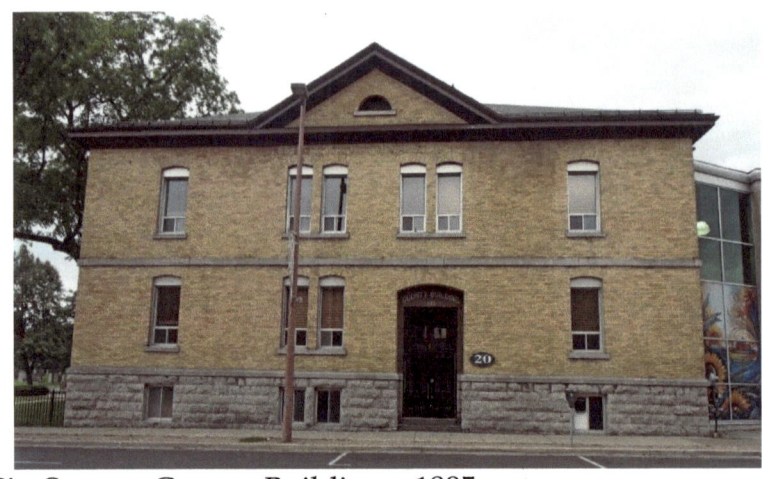

Pitt Street – County Building – 1895 – stone course around building, dormer in roof

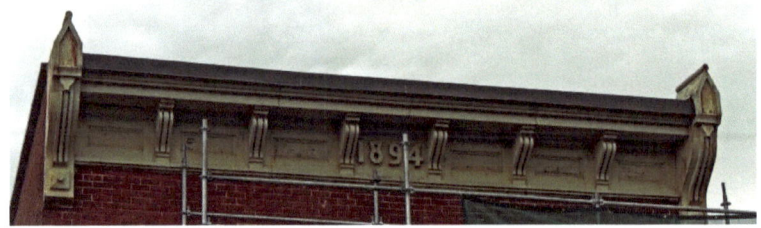

Cornice - 1894

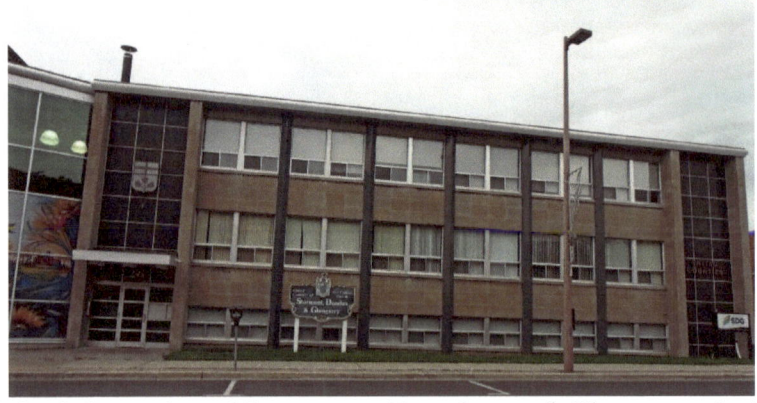

United Counties of Stormont, Dundas and Glengarry is the Eastern Gateway to Ontario; it surrounds the City of Cornwall and its border to the south is the St. Lawrence River.

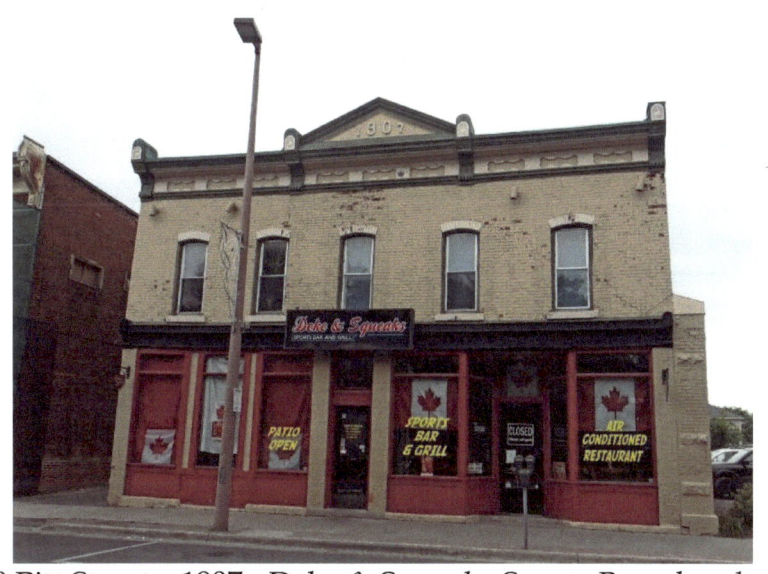

58 Pitt Street – 1907 - Deke & Squeaks Sports Bar – brackets and decorative cornice, Jacobean gable with date

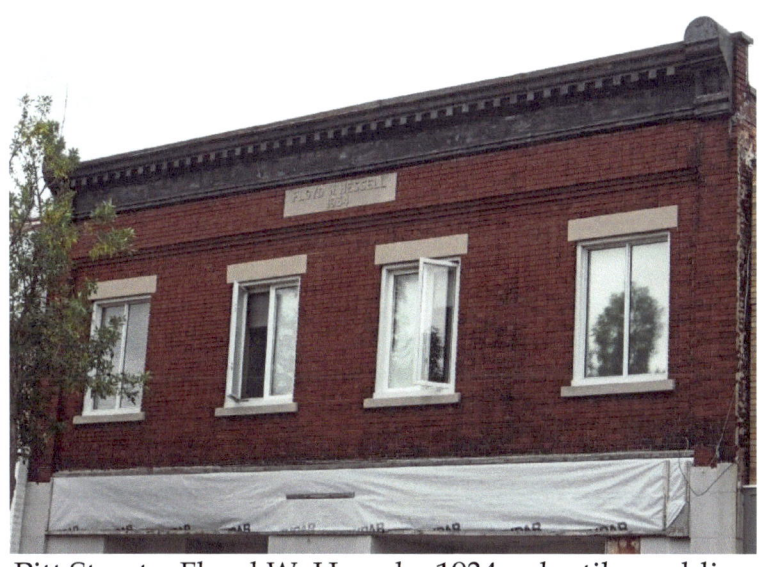

Pitt Street – Floyd W. Hessel – 1934 – dentil moulding

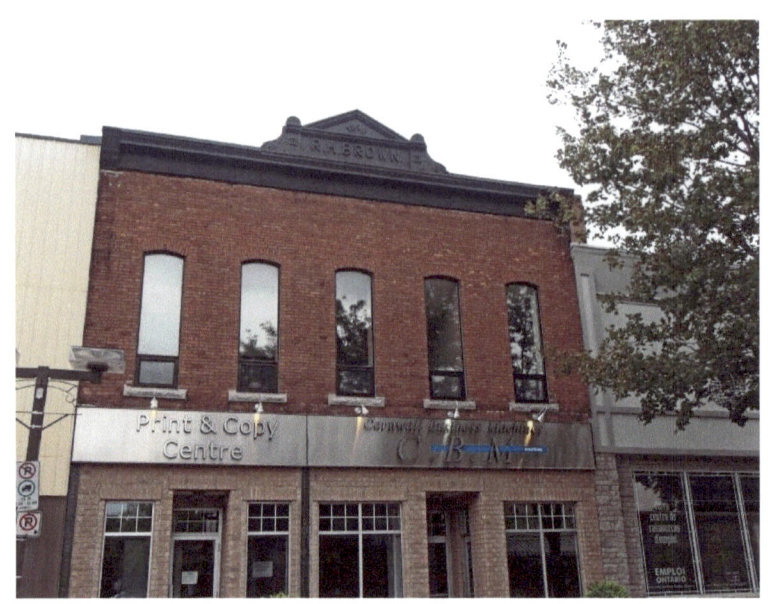

136 Pitt Street - R. H. Brown Block – 1898 – Jacobean gable

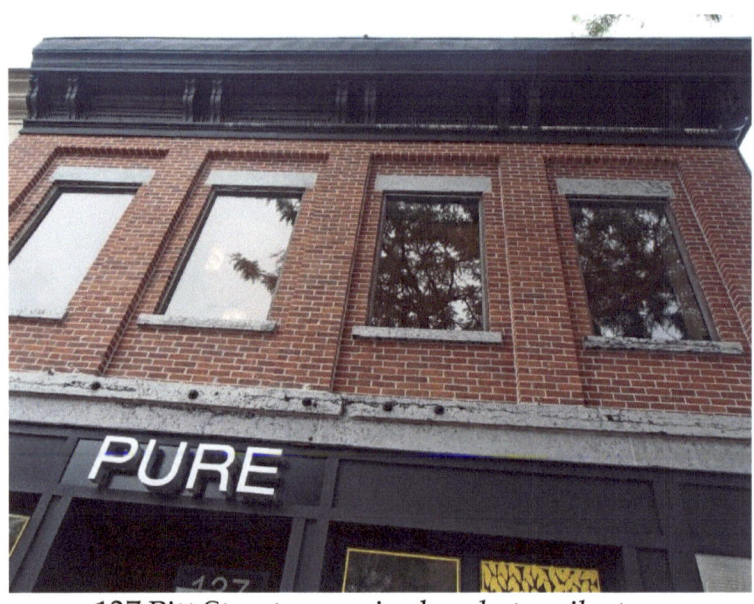

137 Pitt Street – cornice brackets, pilasters

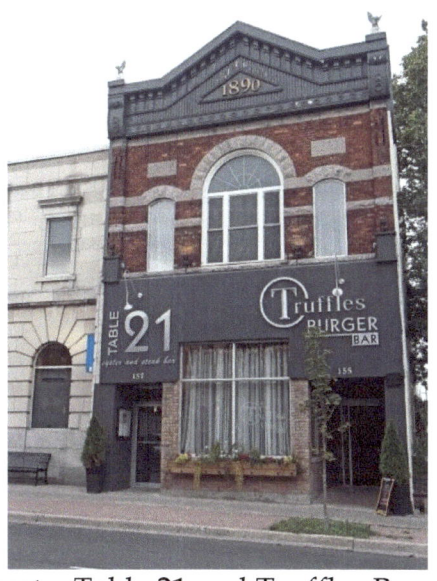

155-157 Pitt Street – Table 21 and Truffles Burger Bar – 1890 –
Jacobean Gable with date and dentil moulding; stone courses

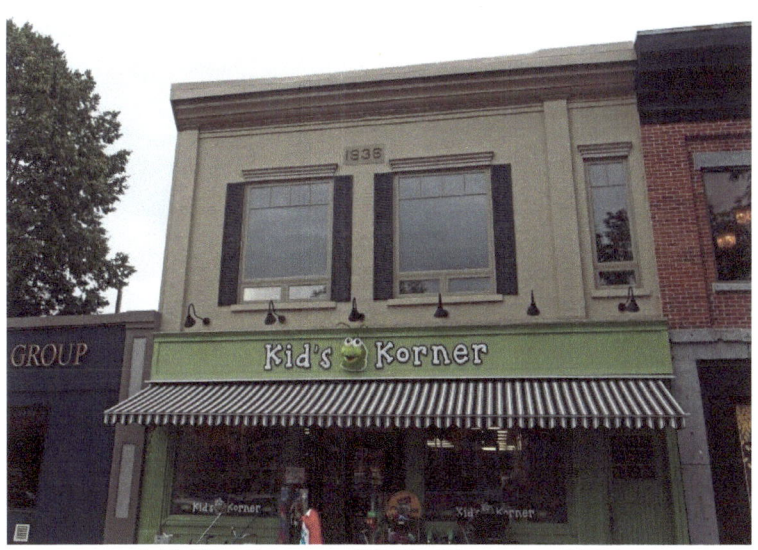

141 Pitt Street – Kid's Korner - 1936

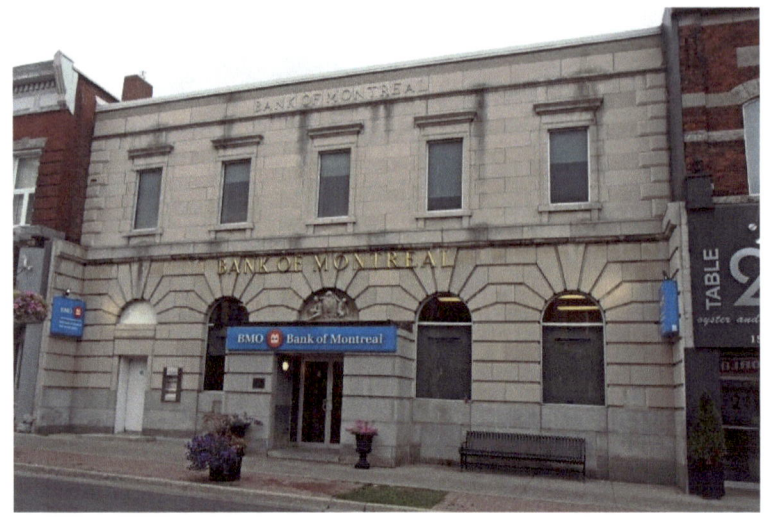

159 Pitt Street - Bank of Montreal – plain window hoods on second storey; decorative stone work on first storey

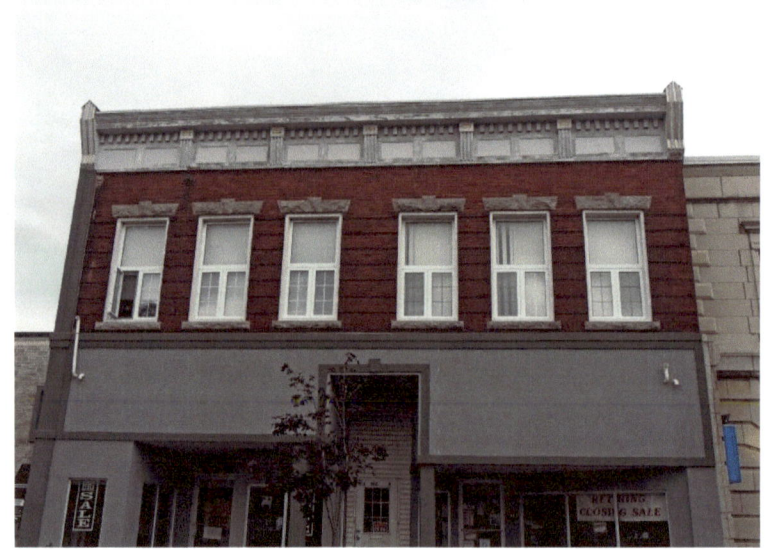

165-167 Pitt Street – decorative cornice with brackets and dentil moulding; stone lintels on brick building

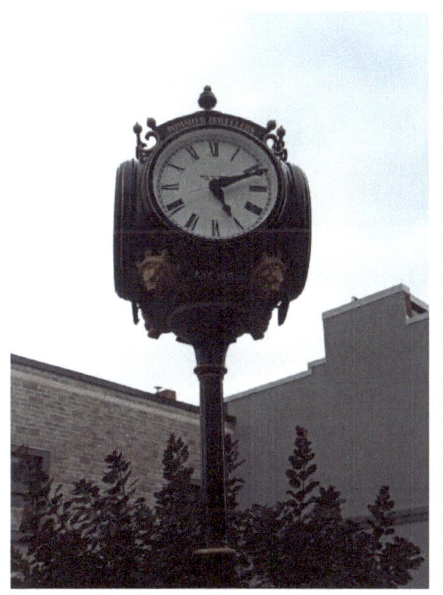

Pommier Jewellers Clock
Established 1937

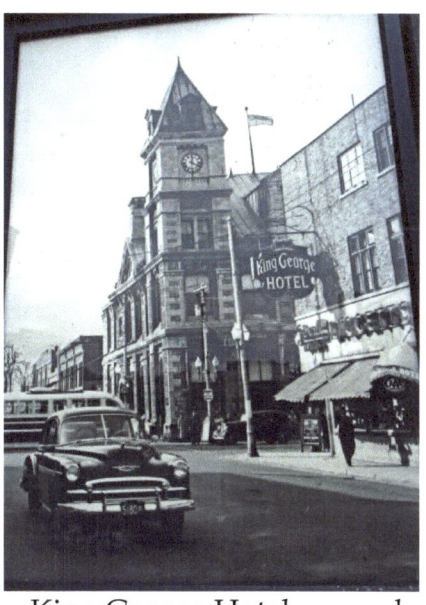

King George Hotel – mural
built in 1825; destroyed by
fire in 1997

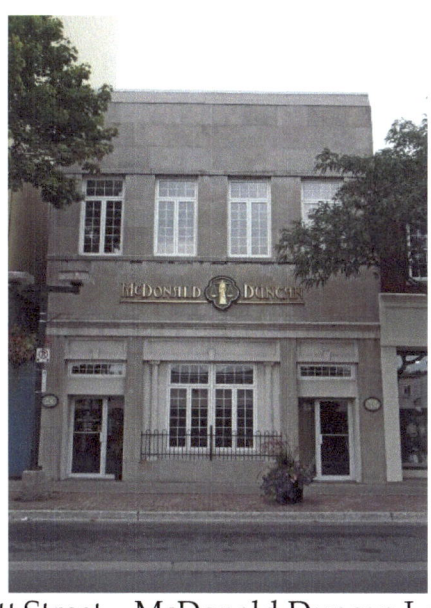

206-208 Pitt Street – McDonald Duncan Law Office –
keystones, engaged Doric columns

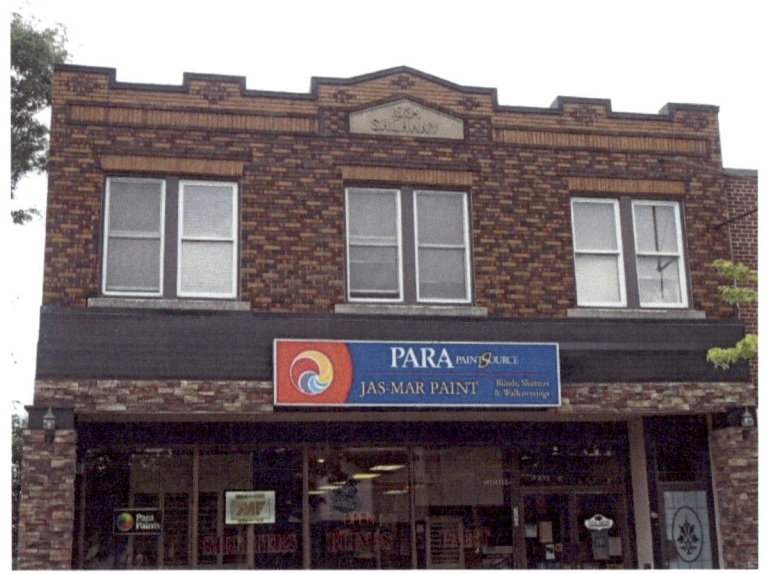

240 Pitt Street – Salhany – 1934 - battlemented rooftop; polychromatic brickwork

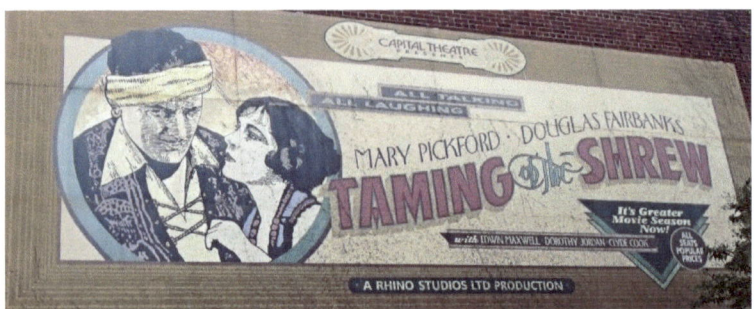

The Capitol Theatre mural across from George Assaly Lane on Pitt Street – The theatre was quite grand and featured movies for many years. The mural depicts the "Taming of the Shrew" featuring Canada's Mary Pickford and Douglas Fairbanks. Over the years, the theatre hosted theatre productions, movies, concerts, high school graduation ceremonies, dance recitals, and choir productions. The site now houses the provincial courthouse.

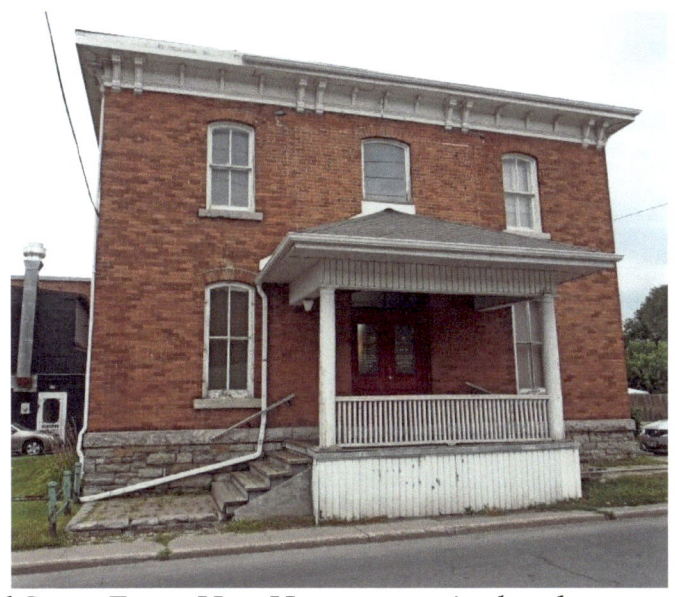

5 Third Street East – Hart House – cornice brackets, voussoirs, porch posts with Doric capitals, open railing

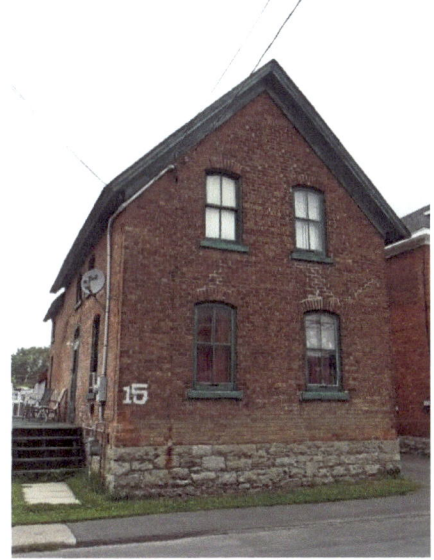

15 Third Street East
Voussoirs, cobblestone
foundation

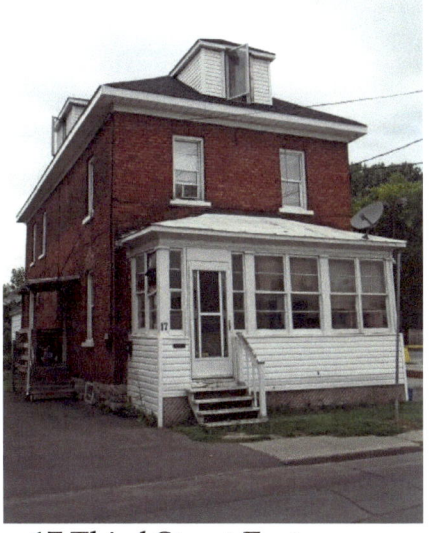

17 Third Street East
dormers, enclosed front
porch

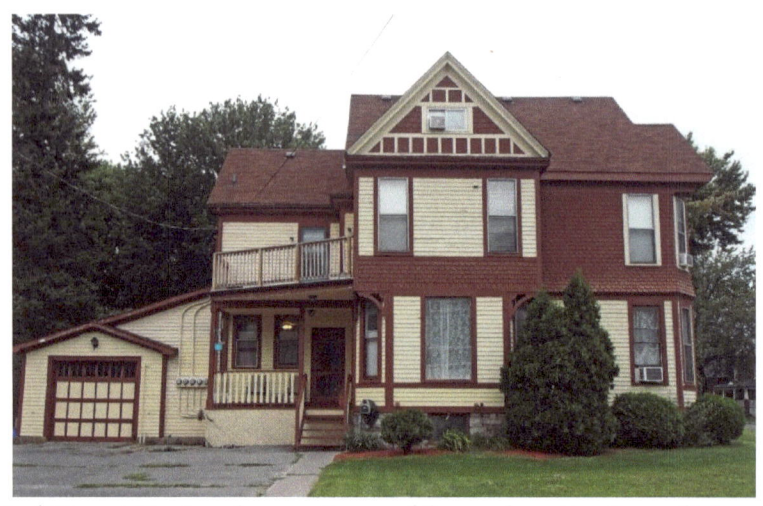

Third Street East – decorative gable on frontispiece, fish scale patterning, fretwork; second floor balcony

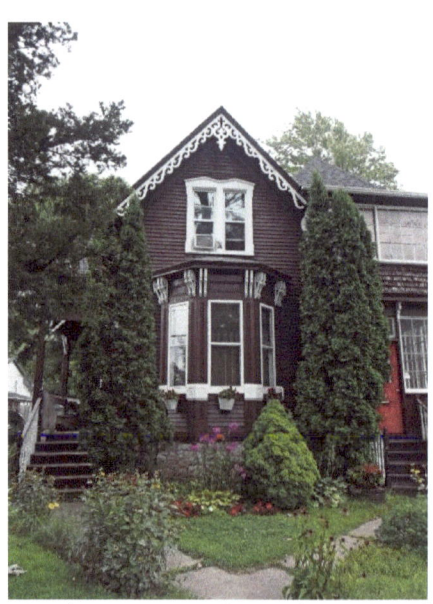

Sydney Street – Gothic – verge board trim and finial on gable; bay window with cornice brackets

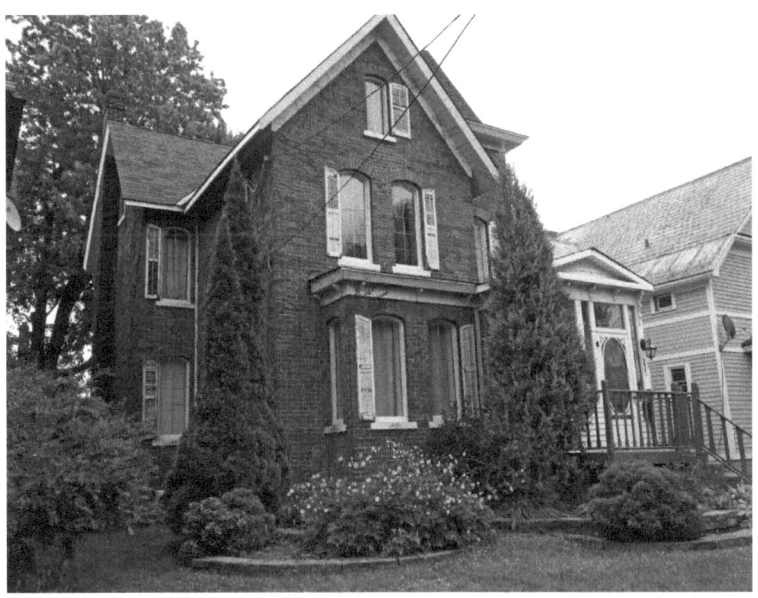

237 Sydney Street – Gothic – rectangular bay window; enclosed porch with cornice brackets and pediment

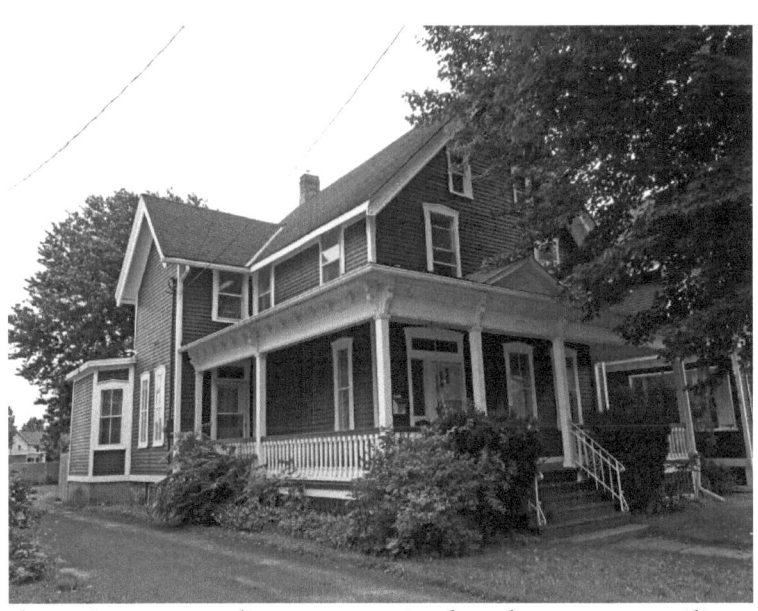

Sydney Street – pediment, cornice brackets, open railing on wraparound verandah; sidelight, transom

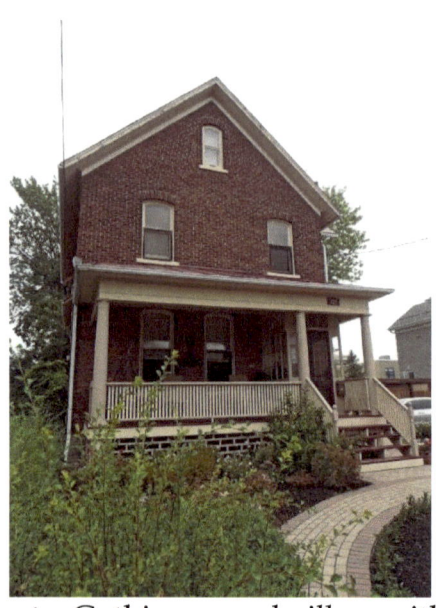

225 Sydney Street – Gothic – round pillars with Doric capitals supporting verandah with open railing

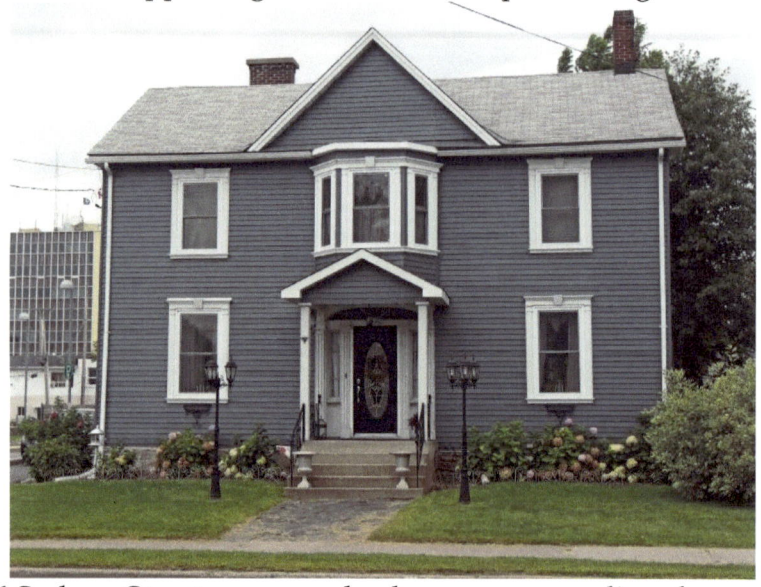

226 Sydney Street – engaged columns surrounding door with sidelights, transom; pediment above porch; oriel window with gable above

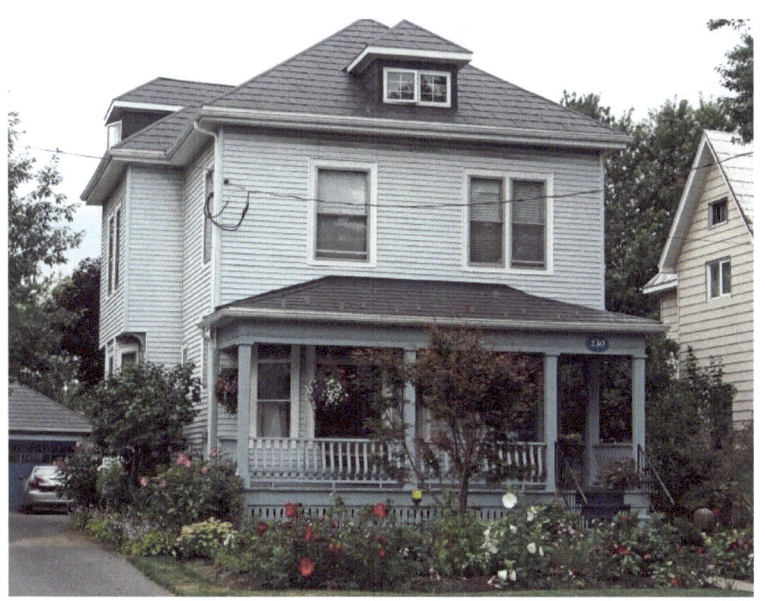

230 Sydney Street – dormers in hipped roof; square pillars supporting verandah with open railing

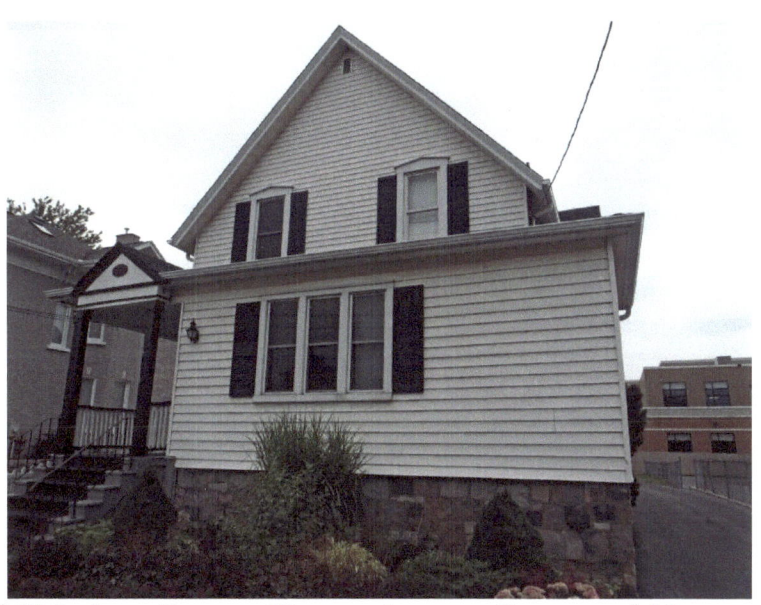

215 Sydney Street – Vernacular – pediment, cobblestone foundation

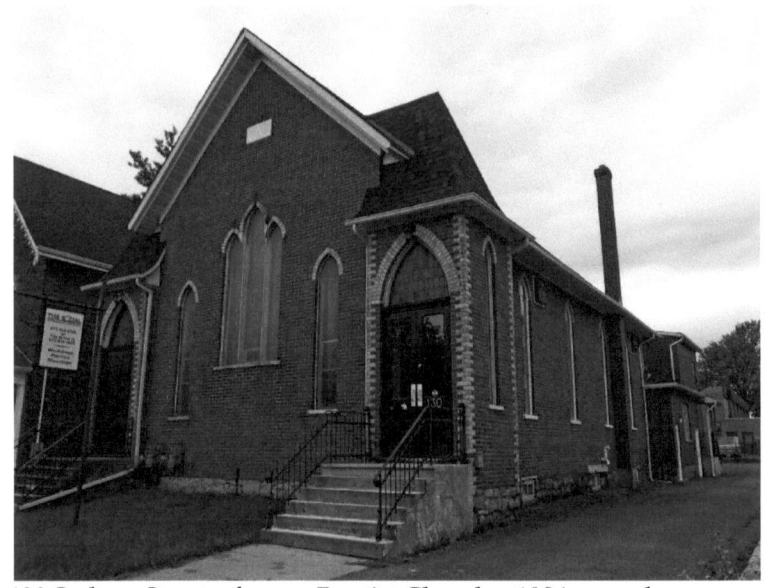

130 Sydney Street - former Baptist Church – 1884 - rough masonry (cobblestone) foundation, brick building - Gothic style - steeply pitched roof, narrow pointed lancet windows, the use of multi-colored brick to accentuate the pointed arches over the door and windows, corner quoins

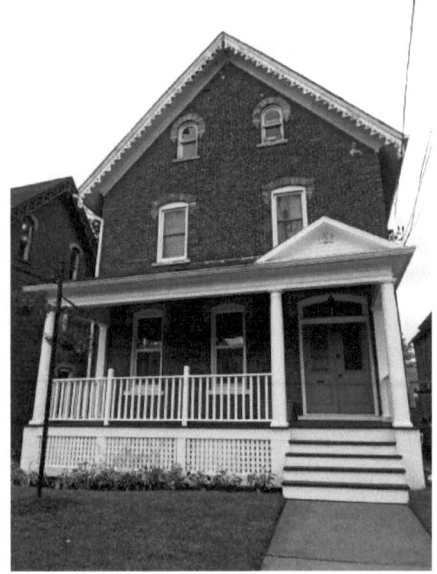

126 Sydney Street – verge board trim on gable, voussoirs, pediment, Doric pillars supporting verandah with open railing; transom window

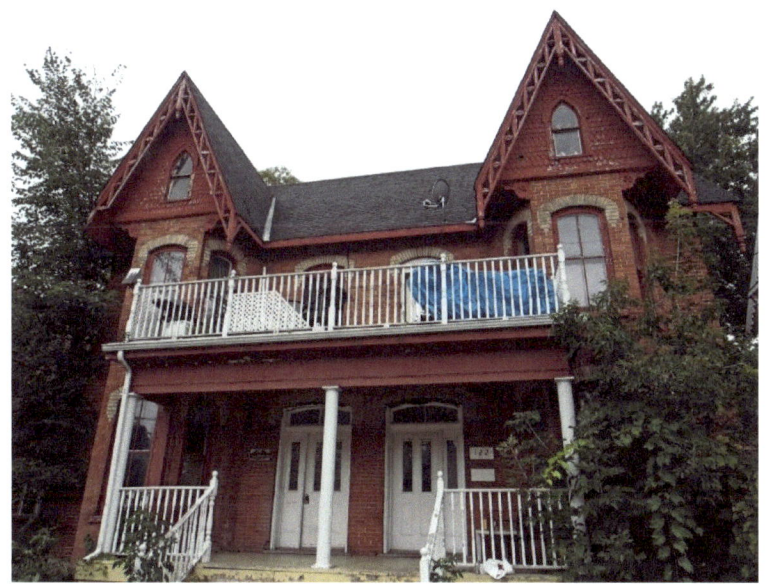

120-122 Sydney Street – Gothic Revival – verge board trim with finials on gables; fretwork; voussoirs; second floor balcony with open railing

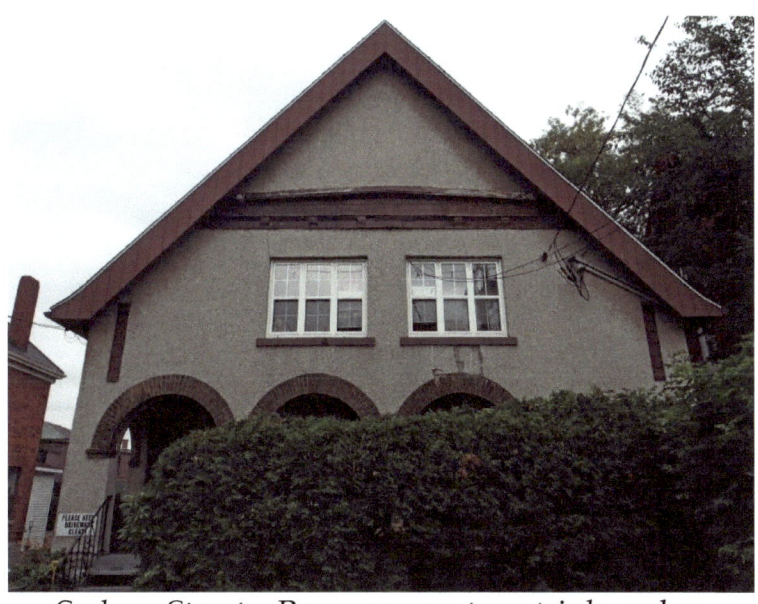

Sydney Street – Romanesque-type triple arches

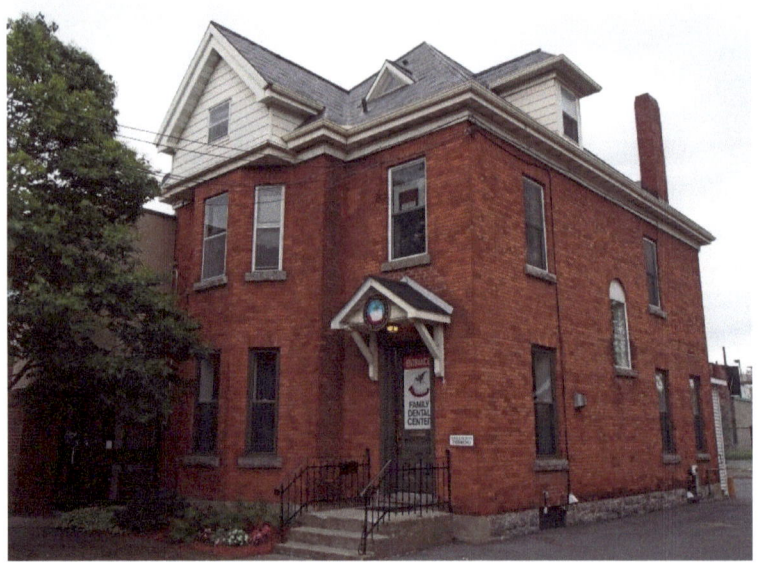

110 Sydney Street – dormers, frontispiece

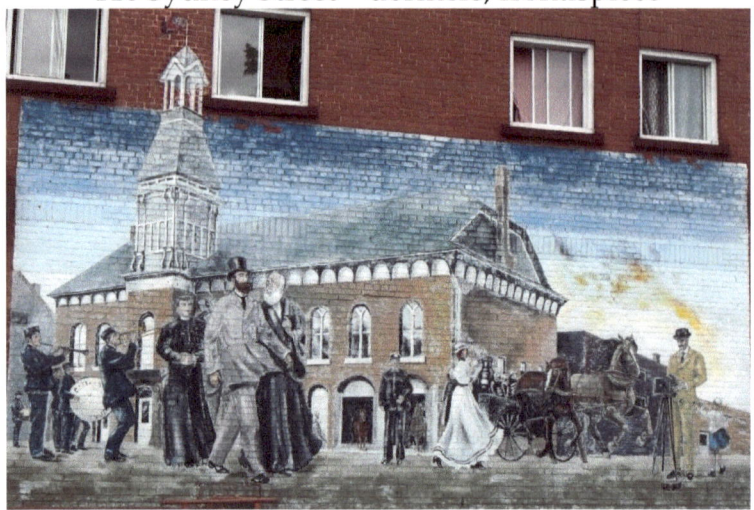

The Old Town Hall 1900 mural on Pitt and Third Streets across from the Royal Bank – Cornwall purchased its first fire engine in 1832; in 1888 the city invested in fire hydrants and water works; by 1900 the fire brigade had four stations and twenty men; the citizens' band performed from 1886 to 1905 as street entertainment.

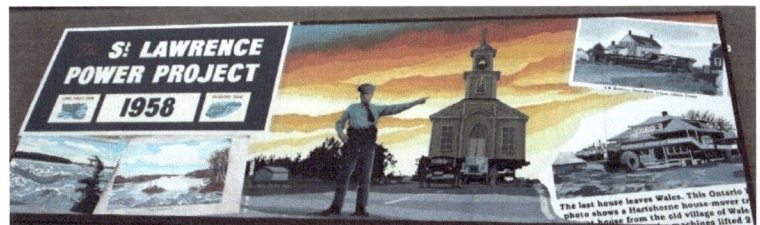

The Seaway City mural between First and Second Streets on Pitt Street – The early years feature river transportation with timber rafts and lake boats running the Long Ault rapids; later the canal was an integral part of the city; in the 1950s the seaway was flooded destroying six villages and three hamlets west of the city; the flooding created the head pond for the international dam and the creation of the St. Lawrence Seaway; Christ Church was moved from Moulinette to Upper Canada Village.

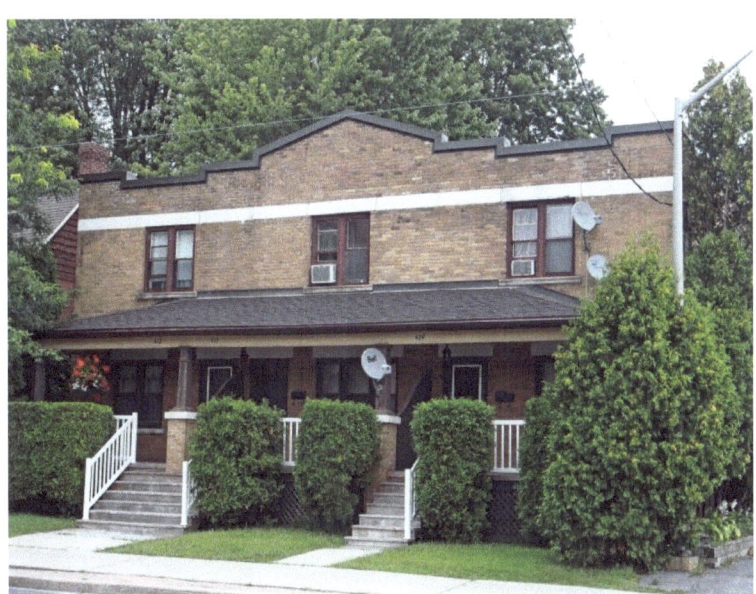

409-413 Pitt Street – battlemented roofline with Jacobean gable, banding above second floor windows

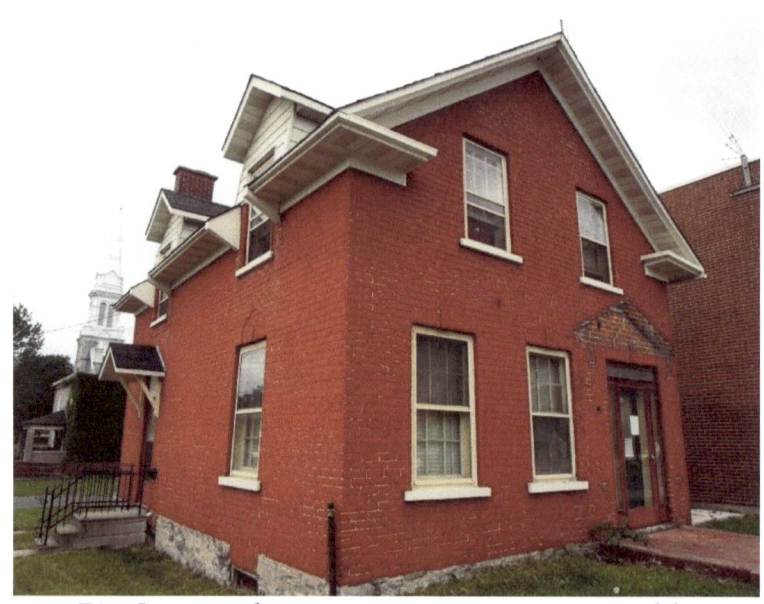

Pitt Street – dormers, cornice return on gable

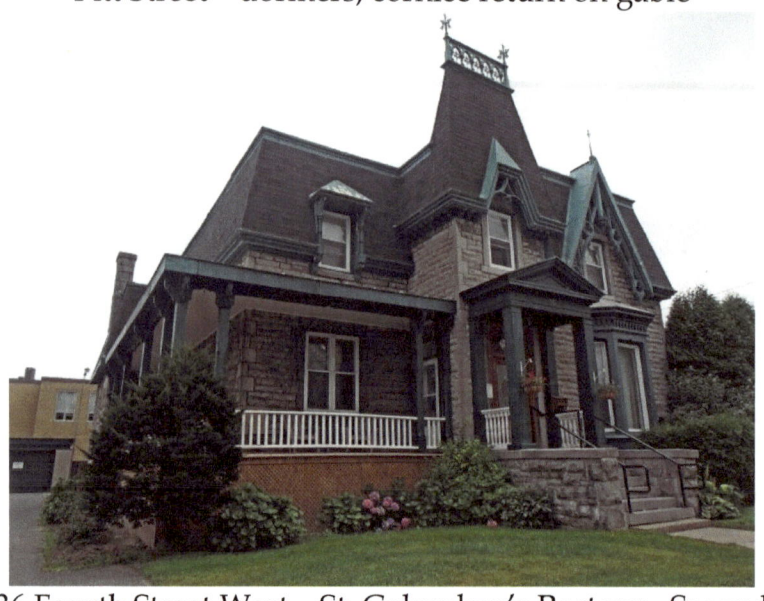

36 Fourth Street West – St. Columban's Rectory - Second
Empire domestic architecture with mansard roof and
detailing; window hood, trim on gable, bay window, cornice
brackets; open railing on porch and wraparound verandah

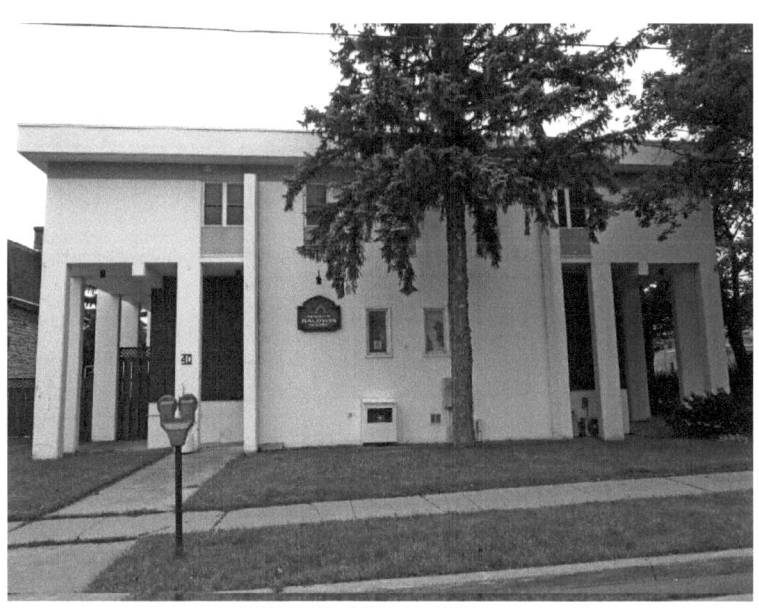

#40 – Baldwin House

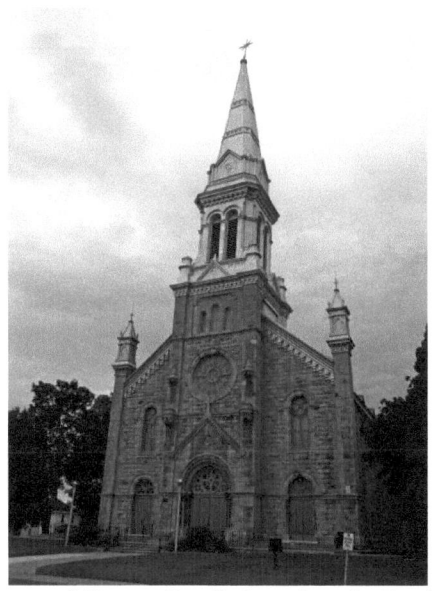

40 Fourth Street West - St. Columban's Parish Church -
Founded in 1829, this was the first Roman Catholic Church to
be established in Cornwall

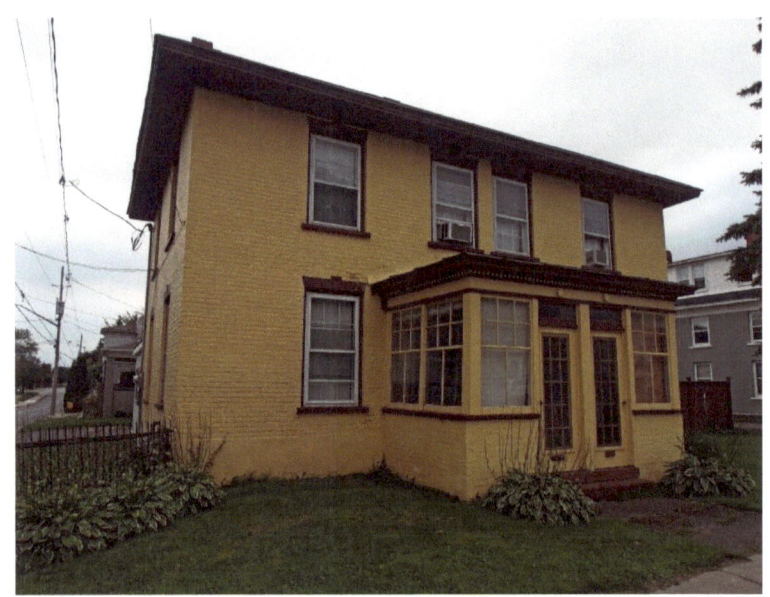

Voussoirs with keystones, dentil moulding on closed porch

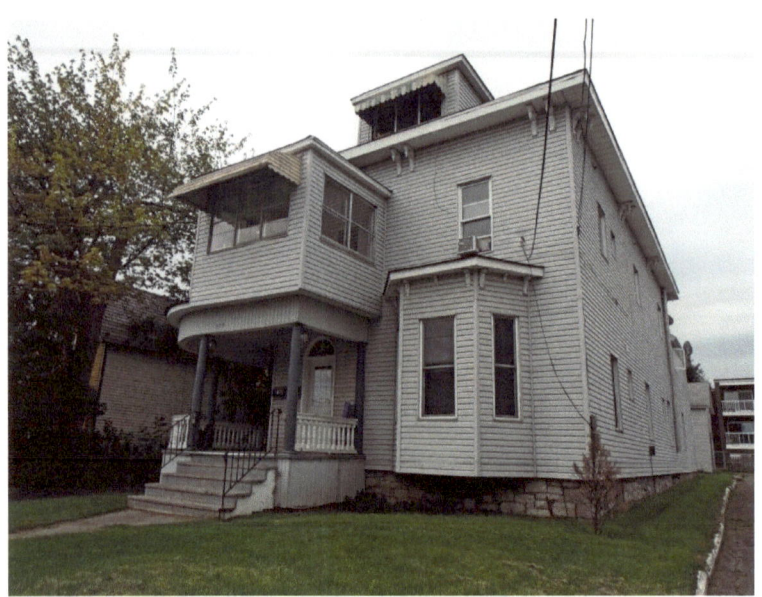

320 Augustus Street – dormers, bay window with cornice brackets

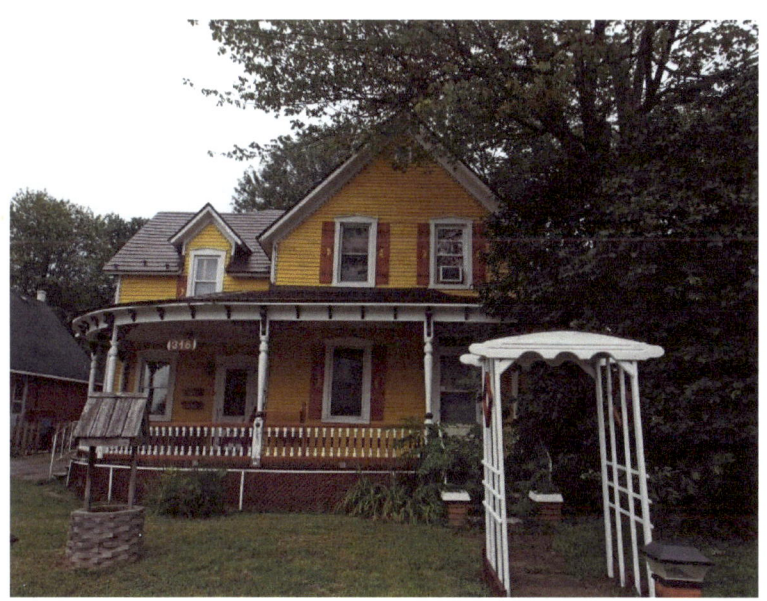

318 Augustus Street – Gothic Revival – wraparound verandah with cornice brackets, turned spindle supports, and open spindle railing

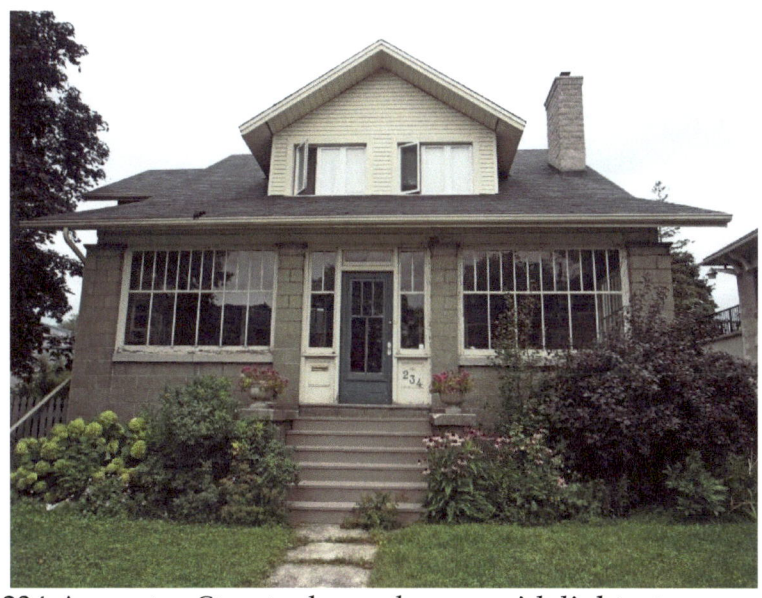

234 Augustus Street – large dormer; sidelights, transom

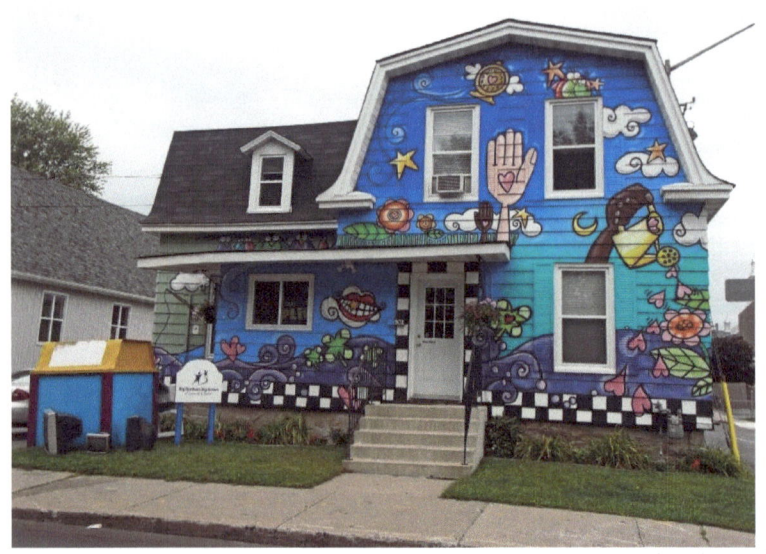

101 Third Street West – Neo-colonial style – gambrel roof, dormer

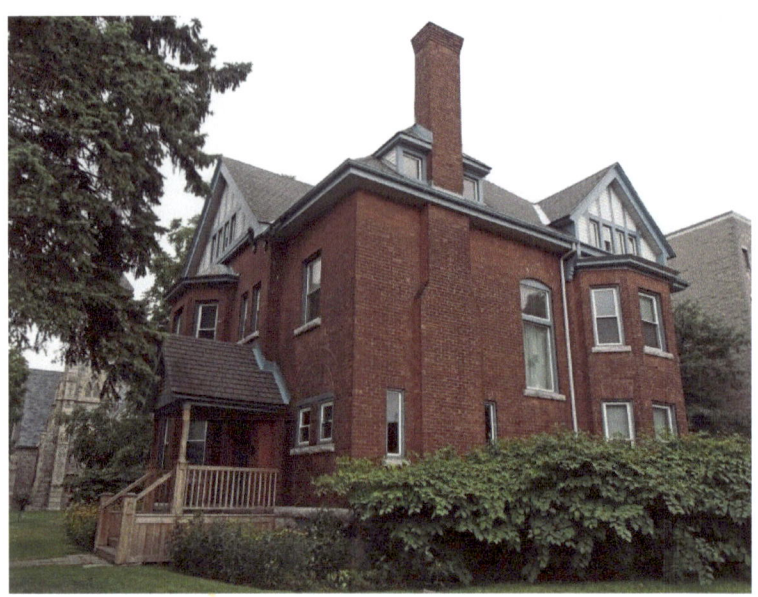

Second Street West – Tudor half-timbering on gables, cornice brackets; decorative brickwork; two-storey bay windows

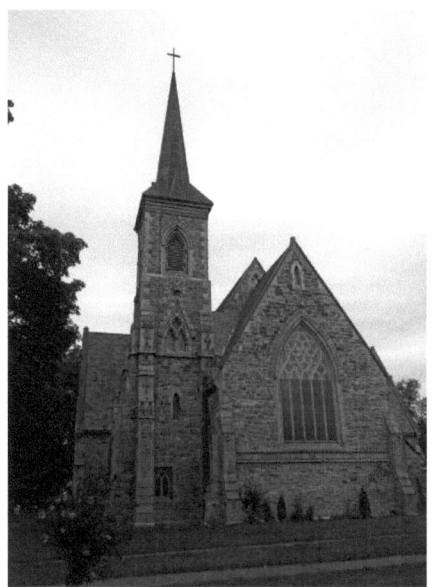

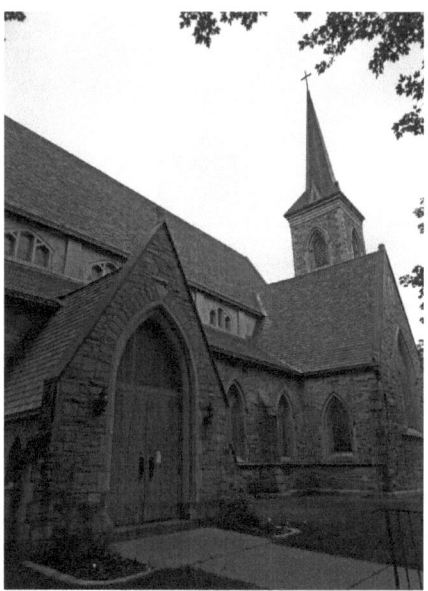

105 Second Street West - Trinity Anglican Church
Gothic Revival – lancet windows; buttresses; quatrefoil
designs; string course below large window

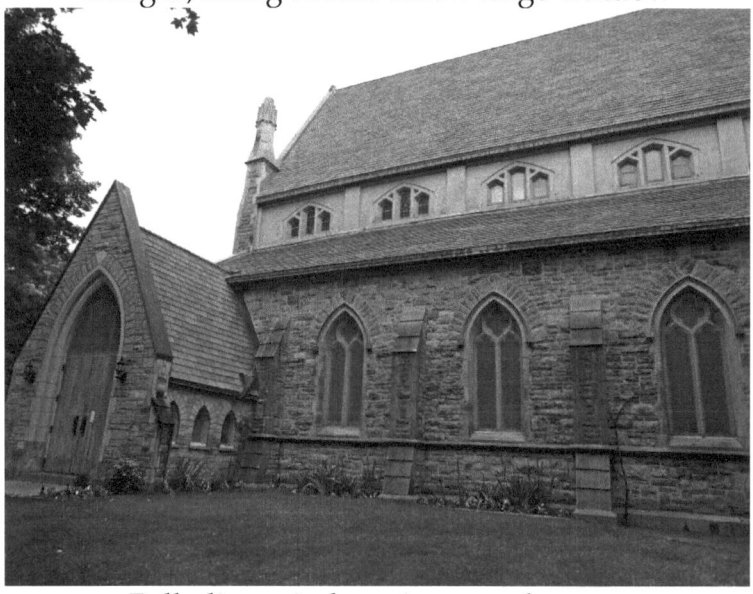

Palladian windows in second storey

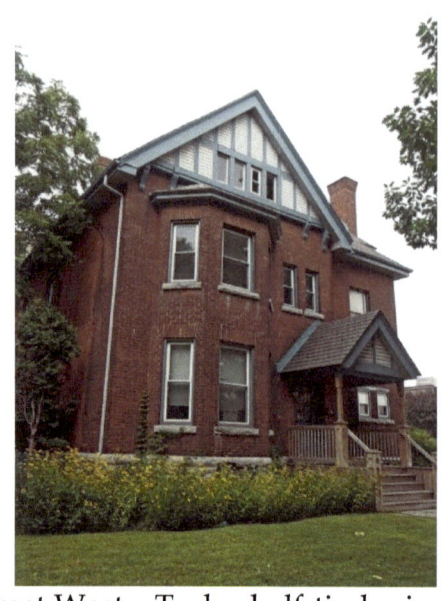

101 Second Street West – Tudor half-timbering in gable; two-storey bay window; pediment; turned wooden porch supports with open railing

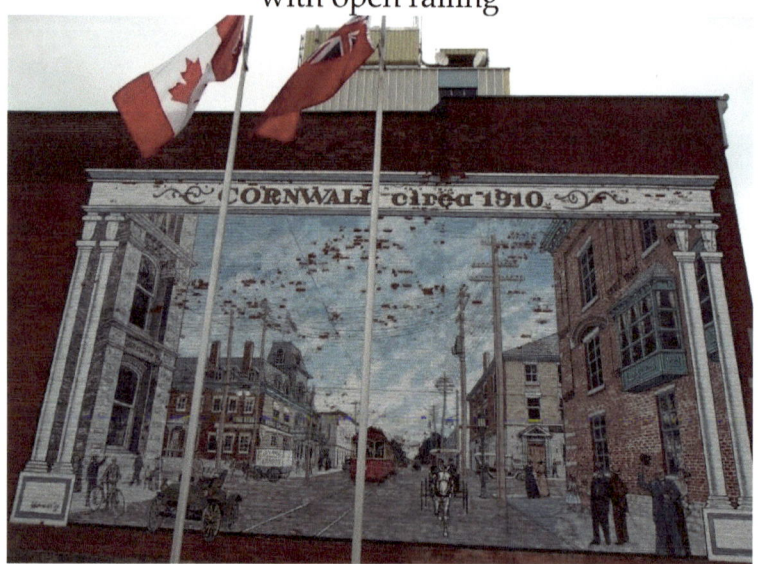

Cornwall Circa 1910 mural Second Street West next to Courthouse – shows corner of Pitt and Second Streets; grey building in front was the post office 1833-1955 (demolished to build the Seaway Building

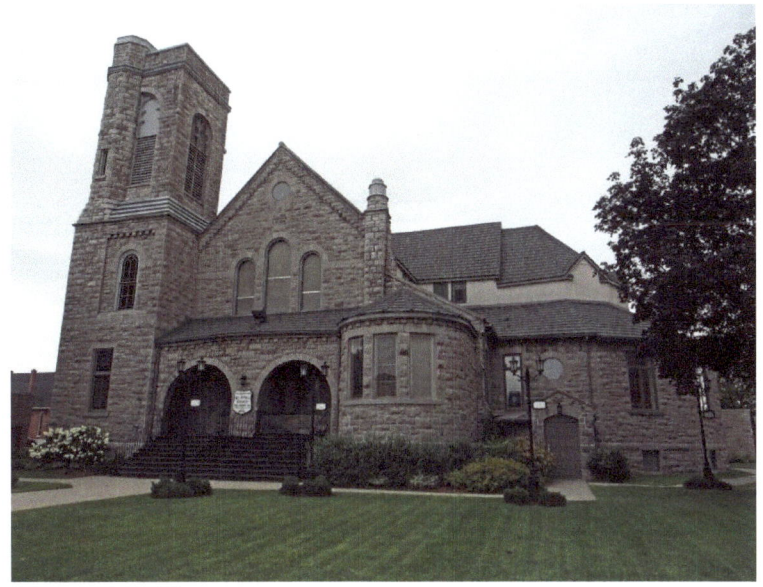

28 Second Street East - St. John's Presbyterian Church – 1888
- Romanesque style – dentil moulding, trefoil decoration on
tower

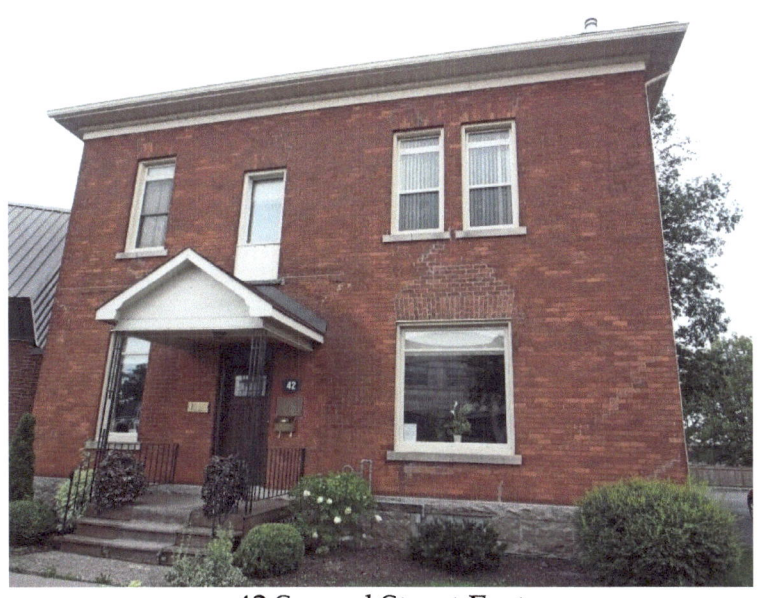

42 Second Street East

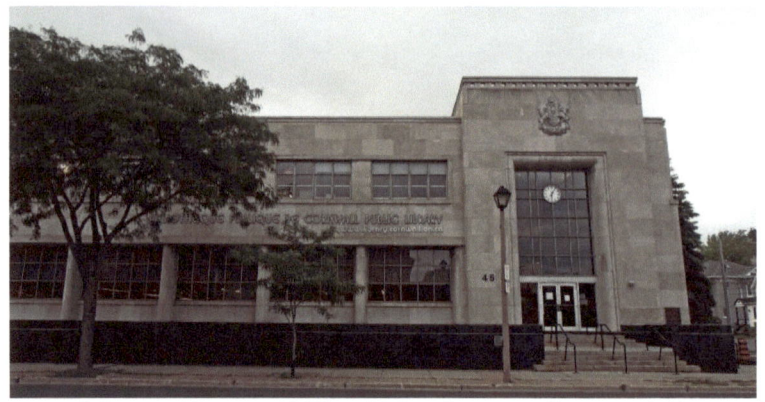

45 Second Street East – 1953-1995 - Cornwall Post Office; when the post office closed, it was renovated and became the Cornwall Public Library - limestone façade and aluminum-framed windows, parapet on top of frontispiece

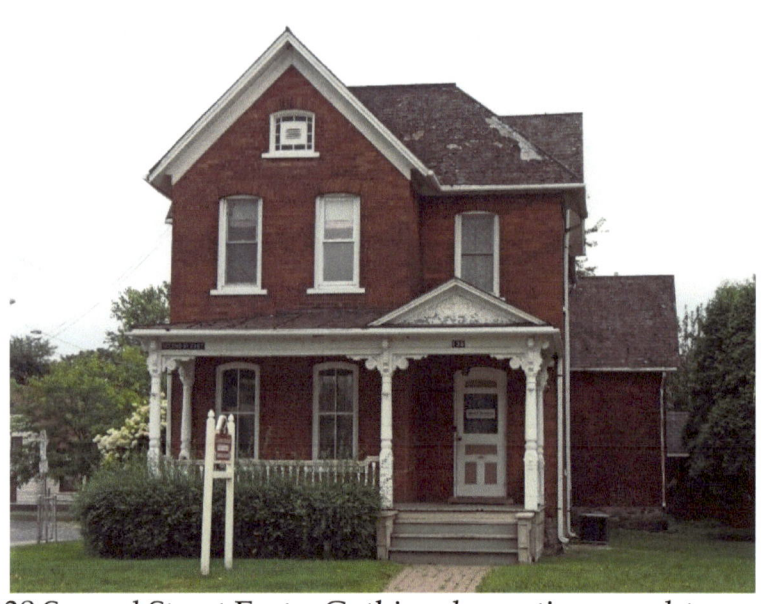

138 Second Street East – Gothic - decorative wood-turned veranda support posts, open railing, pediment with decorative tympanum

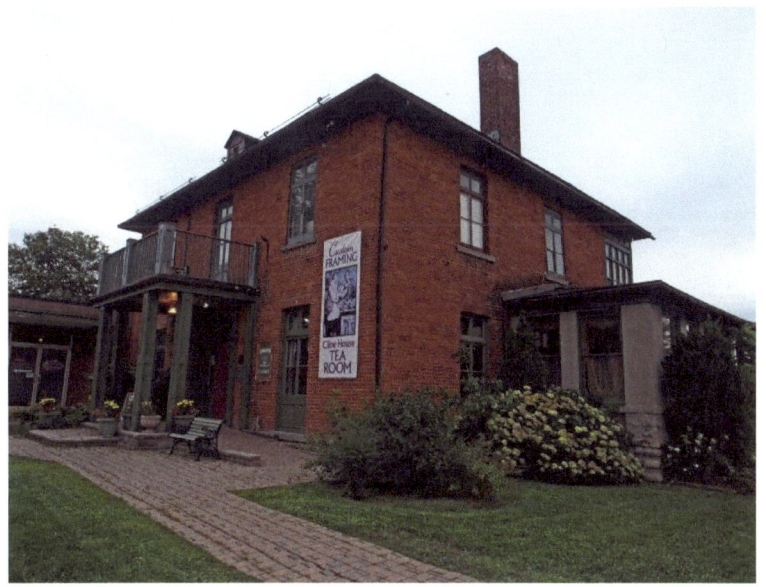

204 Second Street East – Cline House – built late 1850s – Neo-Palladian Georgian home - red brick, symmetrical exterior façades, second floor balcony

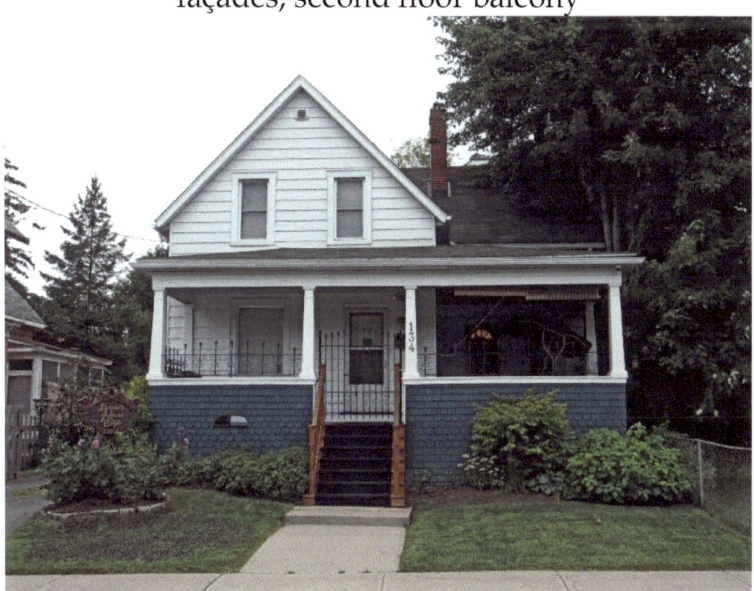

134 Second Street East – Doric capitals on pillars supporting verandah

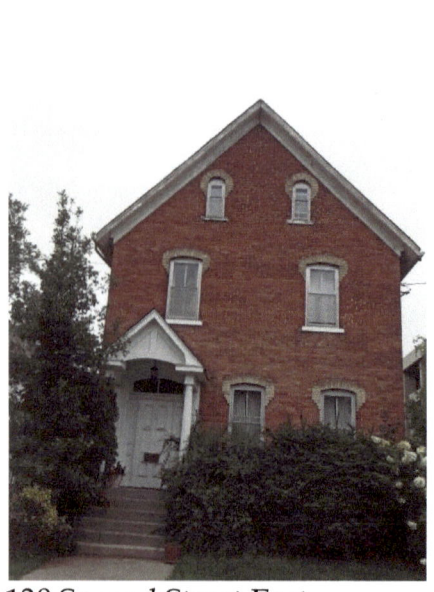

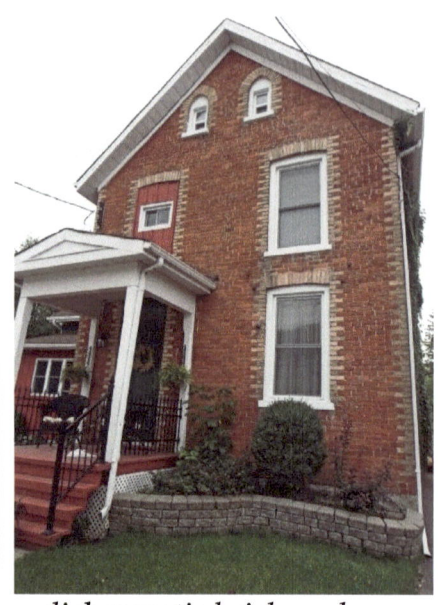

130 Second Street East   dichromatic brickwork
Dichromatic voussoirs   pediment, corner quoins

2½ storeys

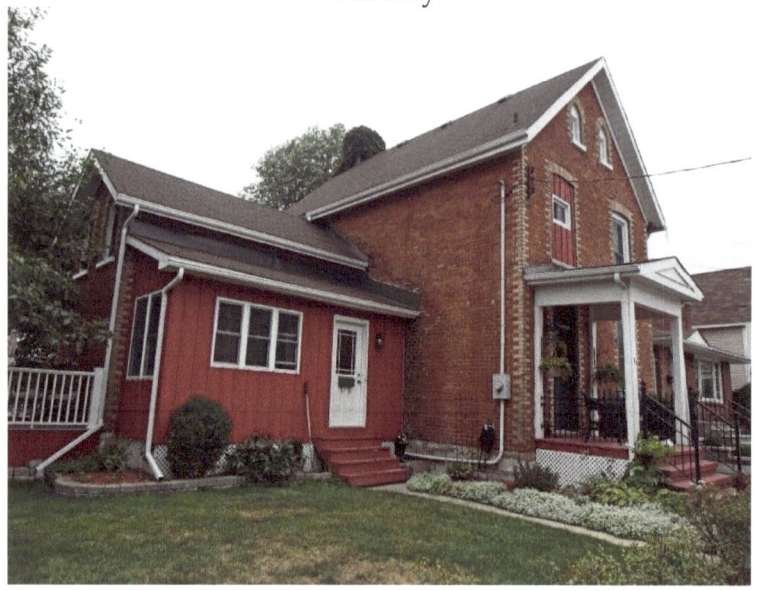

Architectural Terms

Banding: Different materials, colors or textures used in horizontal bands along a wall. Example: 325 Water Street East, Page 11	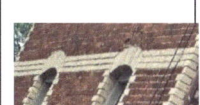
Battlement: A design for a parapet that has alternating solid parts and openings, originally used for defense, but later used as a decorative motif. Example: 500 Montreal Road, Page 20	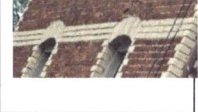
Bay Window: A window that projects out from a wall, in a semicircular, rectangular, or polygonal design. Used frequently in Gothic and Victorian designs. Example: 331 Water Street East, Page 11	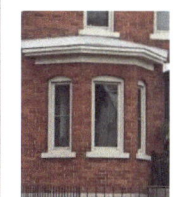
Brackets: a decorative or weight-bearing structural element which forms a right angle with one side against a wall and the other under a projecting surface such as an eave or roof. Example: cornice, page 24	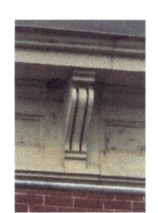
Buttress: a masonry structure built against or projecting from a wall which serves to support or reinforce the wall. In Canadian architecture, they are sometimes used for decoration. Example: 105 Second Street West, Page 45	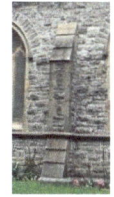

Capital: The uppermost finish or decoration on a column. An Ionic column has a small base, a thin elegant shaft, and a capital composed of volutes which are carved whirls or twists that take the form of a scroll. Example: 300 Montreal Road, Page 17	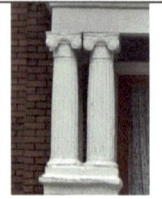 Ionic
A Doric column is characterized by a plain column with no base, a shaft with twenty flutings, and a simple capital with a simple entablature. Example: 126 Sydney Street, Page 36	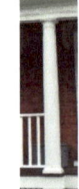 Doric
Cobblestone architecture: Refers to the use of cobblestones embedded in mortar as a method for erecting walls on houses and commercial buildings. Example: 215 Sydney Street, Page 35	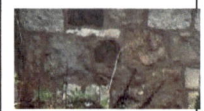
Columns were initially created to support a roof and porch structure. Originally they were free standing. Over time, builders began to build the walls between the columns so that the columns were part of the wall itself. These are called engaged columns. Engaged columns can be either structural or decorative. Example: 226 Sydney Street, Page 34	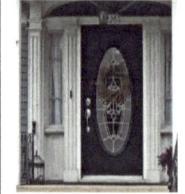
Cornice: originally the wooden overhang of the roof. With the use of stone, brick, iron and steel, the cornice is any horizontal moulded projection at the top of a building. They can be very decorative. Example: 58 Pitt Street, Page 25	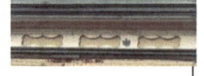

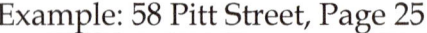

Cornice Return: decorative element on the end of a gable. Example: Pitt Street, Page 40	
Course: continuous horizontal row or layer of stone or brick. Example: Pitt Street, Page 24	
Dentil Moulding: an even series of rectangles used as ornamental decoration in cornices. Example: Pitt Street, Page 25	
Dichromatic brickwork: the use of two colours of brick, tile or slate to decorate a façade. Example: 528 Montreal Road, Page 18	
Dormer: (French for "sleep") a gable end window that pierces through the plane of a sloping roof surface to create usable space in the top floor or attic of a building by adding headroom. Example: 300 Montreal Road, Page 17	
Foil: an architectural device based on a symmetrical rendering of leaf shapes, defined by overlapping circles that produce a series of cusps to make a lobe. The number of cusps can be three (trefoil), four (quatrefoil) or five (cinquefoil), or can be any number (multifoil). Example: 105 Second Street West, Page 45	
Fretwork: interlaced decorative design resembling a bracket Example: Third Street East, Page 32	

Frontispiece: a portion of the façade of a building, usually a centred doorway that is slightly raised from the rest of the building, usually has extensive ornamentation. Frontispieces are usually Classical in design with white columned porches. Example: Third Street East, Page 32	
Gable: the triangular portion of a wall between the edges of a sloping roof. **Jacobean Gable:** the gable extends above the roofline. Example: 155-157 Pitt Street, Page 27	
Gambrel Roof: a symmetrical two-sided roof with two slopes on each side; the upper slope is positioned at a shallow angle, while the lower slope is steep. It is similar to a mansard roof, but a gambrel has vertical gable ends instead of being hipped at the four corners of the building. Example: 101 Third Street West, Page 44	
Hipped Roof: a roof where all sides slope downwards to the walls with no gables. Example: 300 Montreal Road, Page 17	
Keystones and Voussoirs: a voussoir is a wedge-shaped element used in building an arch. A keystone is the central stone that locks all the stones into position, allowing the arch to bear weight. A keystone is often enlarged and embellished. Example: Page 42	

Lancet Window: a tall, narrow window with a pointed arch at its top. Example: 130 Sydney Street, Page 36	
Oriel Window - These small areas were originally set into walls and galleries for the purpose of private prayer. Over time, any projecting window or area on an upper floor was called an oriel. Example: 226 Sydney Street, Page 34	
Palladian Window: a large window that is divided into three sections with the centre section larger than the two side sections and usually arched. Example: 105 Second Street West, Page 45	
Parapet: low wall around the edge of a roof. Example: 45 Second Street East, Page 48	
Pediment: a triangular section above the door or portico, usually supported by columns. The inside of the triangle is called the tympanum. Example: 138 Second Street East, Page 48	
Pilaster: a slightly projecting column built into or applied to the face of a wall for additional structural support. Example: Edward Street, Page 21	

Quoin: masonry blocks at the corner of a wall, often a decorative feature, usually larger or of a different colour than the rest of the wall. Example: Second Street East, Page 50	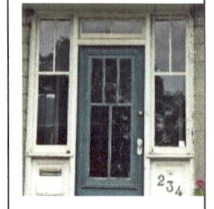
Sidelight: a vertical window that flanks a door, and is often used to emphasize the importance of a primary entrance. **Transom Window:** the light above the doorway, also called a fanlight. Example: 234 Augustus Street, Page 43	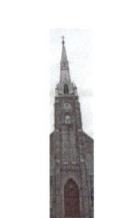
Tower: A circular, square, or octagonal vertical structure higher than the surrounding structure that is usually part of an existing building and is created either for extra defense or for a specific purpose such as a clock or a bell tower. Example: 300 Montreal Road, Page 16	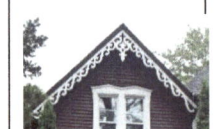
Verge board and Finial: also called bargeboards – hang from the projecting end of a roof and are often elaborately carved and ornamented. **Finial:** ornament added to the top of a gable, pinnacle, canopy or spire – a Gothic element. Example: Sydney Street, Page 32	
Window Hood: A **hood** is the piece found above window openings, usually of an ornate design, and covers the top third of the opening. Hoods are commonly placed above arched or curved openings on both windows and doors. Example: 36 Fourth Street West, Page 40	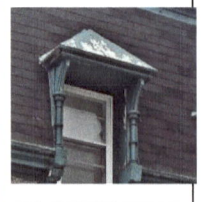

Building Styles

Gothic Revival, 1830-1890 – These decorative buildings have sharply-pitched gables with highly detailed verge boards, pointed-arch window openings, and dichromatic brickwork. It is a common style in Ontario. Example: Sydney Street, Page 32	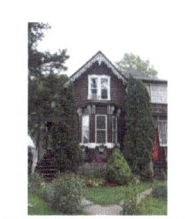
Italianate, 1850-1900 – A two story rectangular building with a mild hip roof, a projecting frontispiece, and generous eaves with ornate cornice brackets was the basis of the style; often there are large sash windows, quoins, ornate detailing on the windows, belvederes and wraparound verandahs. Italianate commercial buildings often have cast iron cresting and elegant window surrounds. Example: 300 Montreal Road, Page 17	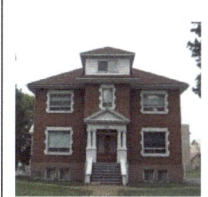
Neo-colonial architecture seeks to revive elements of architectural style of American colonial architecture of the period around the Revolutionary War which drew strongly from Georgian architecture of Great Britain. Architecture from the 18th and early 19th centuries in Ontario includes a wide assortment of detailing and ornament applied to a design centered around the fireplace and the source of water. Structures typically have a symmetrical front facade with elaborate front doorways, often with decorative crown pediments, fanlights, and sidelights, symmetrical windows flanking the front entrance, often in pairs or threes, and columned porches. Example: 101 Third Street West, Page 44	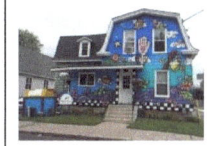

Palladian architecture is a European style derived from and inspired by the designs of the Venetian architect Andrea Palladio (1508–1580). Palladio's work was based on the symmetry, perspective and values of the formal classical temple architecture of the Ancient Greeks and Romans. The style continued to develop from the 17th century until the end of the 18th century. Example: 204 Second Street East, Page 49	
Romanesque Revival, 1880-1910 – This style hearkens back to medieval architecture of the 11th and 12th centuries with a heavy appearance, blocky towers and rounded arches. Example: 28 Second Street East, Page 47	
Second Empire, 1860-1880 – The mansard roof is the most noteworthy feature of this style and is evidence of the French origins. Projecting central towers and one or two-storey bays can also be present. Example: 36 Fourth Street West, Page 40	
Tudor Revival – exposed timbers with stucco infill, multi-paned windows. Example: Second Street West, Page 44	
Vernacular/Traditional Mode 1638 - 1950 Influenced but not defined by a particular style, vernacular buildings are made from easily available materials and exhibit local design characteristics. Example: 215 Sydney Street, Page 35	

www.ingramcontent.com/pod-product-compliance
Lightning Source LLC
Chambersburg PA
CBHW040851180526
45159CB00001B/393